Four Years in Europe with Buffalo Bill

SERIES EDITOR
D. Kurt Graham

CHARLES ELDRIDGE GRIFFIN

Four Years in Europe with Buffalo Bill

Edited and with an introduction by Chris Dixon

University of Nebraska Press
Lincoln & London

Support for this volume was provided by a generous
gift from The Dellenback Family Foundation.

© 2010 by the Board of Regents of the
University of Nebraska. All rights reserved.
Manufactured in the United States of America

All images courtesy the
Buffalo Bill Historical Center.

Support for the printing of this
volume was provided by
Jack and Elaine Rosenthal.

Library of Congress Cataloging-in-Publication Data
Griffin, Charles Eldridge.
Four years in Europe with Buffalo Bill / Charles Eldridge Griffin;
edited and with an introduction by Chris Dixon.
p. cm. — (The papers of William F. "Buffalo Bill" Cody)
Originally published: Albia, IA : Stage Pub. Co., 1908.
Includes bibliographical references.
ISBN 978-0-8032-3423-9 (cloth : alk. paper) — ISBN 978-0-8032-3465-9
(pbk. : alk. paper)
1. Buffalo Bill's Wild West Show—History. I. Title.
GV1821.B8G75 2010
791.8'40973—dc22
2010011201

Set in Iowan Old Style by Bob Reitz.

CONTENTS

List of Illustrations	vii
Series Editor's Preface	ix
Introduction	xiii
About this Edition	xxvii
Four Years in Europe with Buffalo Bill	1
Appendix: Buffalo Bill's Wild West in Europe, 1902–1906	137
Bibliography	155

ILLUSTRATIONS

1. James Bailey and William Cody, ca. 1901   xxxi
2. Wild West advertising poster with female royal personages   xxxii
3. Wild West advertising poster with male royal personages   xxxiii
4. Entente Cordiale poster from the 1904 French tour   xxxiv
5. Signed photograph of William Cody   7
6. Facsimile of Cody letter to Charles Griffin   8
7. Fred Martin, and George Sanger   9
8. Facsimile of George Sanger letter to Charles Griffin   10
9. Charles Eldridge Griffin   11
10. James Bailey   14
11. Line drawing, *It Was Fun to Watch the Seagulls Dive for Biscuits*   23
12. Line drawing, *All Going Out, Nothing Coming In*   24
13. Frederick Bailey Hutchinson   30
14. Paris office and advance staff   37
15. George Starr, and Jule Keene   38
16. Petticoat Lane, London, and Bostock's Hippodrome, Paris   42
17. The Wild West in Paris, 1905   70

18. Entrance to the Wild West, Champs de Mars,
    Paris, 1905 — 72
19. The Wild West in Rouen, 1905 — 80
20. A group of Senegalese, and a mother and son,
    Orléans, 1905 — 84
21. The Tragedie des Chevaux, and a sad farewell — 88
22. Line drawing, *A Visit to Chateau d'If—Monte Cristo
    Island* — 94
23. Line drawing, *In Winter Quarters, Marseilles, 1905–6* — 96
24. Line drawing, *Working under the Southern Sun,
    December, 1905* — 97
25. Winter quarters at Marseille, France (1905) — 99
26. The staff in winter quarters, and Cody's
    two favorite horses — 100
27. The office at winter quarters in Marseille,
    and F. B. Hutchinson having a go at lawn tennis — 101
28. Line drawing, *Street Scene, Genoa, Italy, March, 1906* — 104
29. Opening day in Rome, March 22, 1906 — 108
30. A bunch of the Wild West, photograph taken in
    the old Colosseum, Rome — 110
31. Line drawing, *The Royal Family's Visit to the Wild
    West at Rome, Italy, 1906* — 112
32. The sideshow, 1906 — 116
33. Sioux Indians, and Johnny Baker and Dollie, the
    laughing horse — 118
34. Opening day in Genoa, and double-deck tramcar
    used in England — 120

SERIES EDITOR'S PREFACE

Four years ago the McCracken Research Library in Cody, Wyoming, set out to edit and publish the collected papers of William F. "Buffalo Bill" Cody. It seemed like an idea whose time had come; in fact, it seemed long overdue. William F. Cody was the most famous American of his time. As a cultural figure his influence was unparalleled. And yet, Cody's role in our national narrative is largely underappreciated. As Gretchen Adams, the senior editor of this documentary editing project, has stated, "The Papers of William F. Cody documents the life and times of not one but two men: William Cody and Buffalo Bill. When Cody died in 1917, his public persona so completely eclipsed the identity of the man who created it that they may have buried the body of William F. Cody, but the funeral itself was for Buffalo Bill." Indeed the familiar Buffalo Bill is perhaps viewed today as a quaint character, if not caricature, whose image obscures the substantive William F. Cody. Because Cody is surrounded by so much myth and lore, it is often difficult to trace the very real contribution that he made to the development of the American West.

By publishing William F. Cody's own writings as well as contemporary accounts about him, such as this one by

Charles Eldridge Griffin, the Cody Papers will reveal the man behind the character and the character behind the man. This present volume in particular illustrates that Buffalo Bill's Wild West was the point where man and myth intersected. In the editing of this volume, Chris Dixon has given us an annotated edition that will enhance both the reading experience and classroom use. He has also updated the names of all of the locations where Buffalo Bill's Wild West appeared, which is extremely helpful, given the way the map of Europe has changed since Cody's time. Dixon's careful work brings a little-known writing into circulation and is a tremendous resource for scholars and interested readers at all levels. The Dixon edition of the Griffin volume is a fitting beginning for The Papers of William F. Cody.

One of the major objectives of the project is to collect materials that document the personal and professional life of a man who had thousands of employees, friends, and customers who wrote to him and about him. In addition to the print edition of the Papers, a key output of the project will be a digital version of this entire corpus of material, complete with authoritative transcriptions, which will be made available through the project website and continually updated as new materials are located.

The creation of this digital collection, which brings together the entire body of research materials related to William F. Cody's personal and professional life, will enable a variety of audiences to consider the impact of William F. Cody the cultural entrepreneur on American life and provide contextualizing documents from other sources, including audio-visual media that exist for the final years of his life.

It will allow more scholars to study the man within his times, will provide new resources to contextualize studies of other regional and national events and persons, and will encourage digital edition visitors to explore and learn more about these vital decades of American expansion and development. The digital edition of the Papers will differ significantly from the print edition by including manuscript materials, photographs, and film and sound recordings, and it will offer navigational and search options not possible in the print edition.

As Griffin's volume reveals, it took many people to make Buffalo Bill's Wild West happen. Likewise, there are many people whose combined efforts have made this documentary project a reality. All of the generous donors and talented scholars who have contributed to the success of this effort will be noted in due course. But in this, the first publication, it is appropriate to acknowledge that big ideas are carried to fruition only by sound and steady leadership. The McCracken Research Library was fortunate at the advent of the papers project that in its board chair it had such a leader. Maggie Scarlett was not only an early supporter of this documentary editing project but also its first true champion. It was through her connections (and tenacity) that the initial funds were raised to launch the project. Whether seeking support from private donors, the Wyoming State Legislature, federal granting agencies, or the United States Congress, Maggie led the charge and thereby secured the future of this worthy endeavor. Thus, this reissue of Griffin's account is a legacy not only to William Cody but also to all of those who have made this effort and the larger undertaking possible. In that spirit, though these pages rightfully belong to Charles Eldridge Griffin and to Mr. Dixon, if this volume were mine to dedicate, it would be to Maggie.

Kurt Graham

INTRODUCTION

Chris Dixon

By any standard Charles Eldridge Griffin was a remarkable man. Author, comedian, conjurer, contortionist, dancer, fire-eater, hypnotist, illusionist, lecturer, magician, newspaper owner, publisher, sword swallower, and yogi: Charles Griffin was also known by the stage names of Monsieur F. Le Costro, Professor Griffin, and the Yankee Yogi.

Charles E. Griffin, as he preferred to style himself, was born June 16, 1859, in St. Joseph, Missouri, and, although his mother, Fanny, was a musician, there was nothing in his family background to suggest the appeal that the circus had for him and his two brothers, Frank and Fred. All three made their living in and around a variety of big tents in the late nineteenth and early twentieth centuries when the circus and sideshow industries were becoming big business in America and beyond. By 1862 the family had moved to Albia, Iowa, where his father, John Griffin, was Monroe County superintendent of schools and later county clerk of the courts. It was the "Hawkeye State" with which Griffin always identified and which he always called home.

The earliest record we have of Griffin as a performer is at the age of sixteen in 1875 when he and his "one man valise troupe" were touring county fairs, school houses, and town halls in the Midwest. This was a challenging apprenticeship for one so young, but it gave Griffin the opportunity to hone the talents that he would later display to larger audiences across the United States and internationally with various companies including most notably the Bob Hunting Circus, the Ringling Brothers Circus Sideshow and, of course, Buffalo Bill's Wild West.

Griffin's first known engagement with a circus company dates from 1881 and was fairly short-lived. He joined the struggling Hilliard and DeMott's Circus as a magician and side show lecturer and remained with them until they folded the following year. He clearly made a strong impression though, because at the tender age of twenty-two he was invited to travel to France and become general manager of the Paris Pavilion Shows. This was Griffin's first notable venture overseas. Little is known about his time in France, but he resurfaced in the United States two years later with Pullman and Mack's Circus, appearing as "The Comic Yankee Conjurer" throughout its brief existence in the 1884–1885 season. The company's demise was not a setback for Griffin, however, and the following year his career went from strength to strength when he joined the famous Sells Brothers Circus as both a fire-eater and a sideshow lecturer.

Griffin's life took a crucial turn in 1886, when he left Sells Brothers to join the newly formed Hurlburt and Hunting Circus in New York City, which later became known as Bob Hunting's New York Circus. During the twelve years that he spent with Hunting, he set up his own New York Conjuring College and added writing and publishing to his growing list of accomplishments. He produced *Griffin's Book of Wonders*, the first of his many instruction manuals for aspiring circus performers, in 1887. A year later, the first of his two memoirs, *Traveling with a Circus: A History of Hunting's N.Y. Cirque Curriculum for Season 1888*, came off the Van Fleet presses in New York. These were followed by booklets on snake charming, using dumb bells, conjuring, how to be a contortionist, fire eating, and his 1897 *The Showman's Book of Wonders*, a compendium on "magic, ventriloquism, fire eating, sword swallowing and hypnotism." The multitalented Griffin self-published all but one of these (*Satan's Supper, or, Secrets of a Fire King*) and sold them at the circus for ten cents a copy.

These were fruitful years for Griffin, both professionally and personally. He was variously billed in Hunting's programs as "Professor Griffin, the Yankee Yogi, Magician and Sword Swallower"; as "Illusionist and Ventriloquist"; and as "Manager All Privileges." By 1898 he owned and managed the entire sideshow operation. The previous year, he became part-owner of the *Maquoketa (Iowa) Weekly Excelsior*. It was during this time that he met and married his wife, Olivia, a snake charmer who worked with him on the show.

The Frank A. Robbin's Circus recruited Griffin to run its sideshows in 1898, but he remained with them for only one season. Griffin spent the next four years from 1899 to 1902 with the Ringling Brothers Circus Side Show based in Baraboo, Wisconsin, as both stage manager and entertainer in his own right, performing magic, ventriloquism, and sword swallowing, as well as lecturing.

In June 1902, when the Ringling Circus appeared in

Canton, Ohio, the renowned James A. Bailey of Barnum and Bailey fame, who was by that time a partner in Buffalo Bill's Wild West, made what Griffin described as an unprecedented visit to a rival circus with the objective of recruiting performers for the Wild West's forthcoming tour of Europe.[1] Griffin was one of those that Bailey approached, and on March 28, 1903, accompanied by his wife and son, he set sail for Liverpool aboard the Cunard steamer *Etruria*.

Griffin joined the Wild West in Manchester and performed his "Yankee Magic" in the sideshow throughout the remainder of that season. His managerial talents and experience did not go unrecognized, and when Lew Parker decided not to rejoin the show for the 1904 British tour, Griffin replaced him as manager for the Wild West. He stayed in that role through 1905 and 1906, wintering in Europe when many of the other leading figures returned to the United States for the off seasons. He travelled with the Wild West across France, Italy, Germany, Belgium, and Luxembourg, and to various parts of central and eastern Europe which, at that time, came under the single banner of the Austro-Hungarian Empire and encompassed present-day Austria, Croatia, the Czech Republic, Hungary, Poland, Romania, Serbia, Slovenia, and the Ukraine.

Upon his return to the States in October 1906, Griffin settled in his old home town of Albia, Iowa, and began writing *Four Years in Europe with Buffalo Bill* (1908), his second memoir and the work for which he is best known among Cody scholars. The book took Griffin two years to complete due in part to ill health, as he suffered a mild stroke in late

1906, and also in part to his professional commitments, as he rejoined the Wild West for the 1907 season as manager and side show artist. This was his final curtain call as a performer, if we discount occasionally entertaining his neighbors with performances at Albia's Opera House in the closing years of his life. The first—and so far only—edition of *Four Years in Europe with Buffalo Bill*, was published under the imprint of Griffin's own Stage Publishing Company, which he had acquired around the turn of the century. Its print run was a mere five hundred copies.

Although eclectic in nature, as memoirs often are, Griffin's direct and at times almost conversational style is engaging throughout. He tells us early in the work that his intention is not "to tire the reader with useless verbiage or dry statistics [. . . . . .] but to give a straightforward narrative of the many interesting places visited, and the *contretemps* met with in such a stupendous undertaking."[2] It is an intention that he meets admirably.

Writing and publishing remained the primary focus of Griffin's activities for the rest of his life. He continued to produce guides for aspiring performers on Black Face Monologue, contortionism, fire eating, juggling and balancing, magic cauldron and magic kettle acts, rope and wire walking, stage dancing, and ventriloquism—each available by mail order for $1.00, postage paid, from his Albia base. He even produced his own (almost certainly bootleg) edition of Helen Whetmore Cody's 1899 *Last of the Great Scouts*, which was "expressly printed to commemorate the return from Europe of Colonel Cody and his Rough Riders of the World."[3]

INTRODUCTION xvii

Death came to Charles Eldridge Griffin on January 3, 1914, at his home in Albia in the aftermath of a serious stroke that left him completely debilitated. He had crammed so much into his relatively short life that it is difficult to believe he was only fifty-four years old.

Buffalo Bill's Wild West in Europe

Between 1887 and 1892, and again from 1902 to 1906, Buffalo Bill's Wild West delighted audiences in England, Scotland, Wales, and fifteen other countries in continental Europe with its unbeatable combination of the authentic and the exotic.[4] It was a sensation, igniting "Wild West Fever" by offering what purported to be a genuine experience of the American frontier that people in Europe had previously only ever read or dreamed about.[5]

The Wild West's initial foray to London—where it represented Nebraska at the great American Exhibition of 1887—came at a time when relations between the United States and Britain were not at their best. The strain caused by the War of 1812 and concerns that Britain would recognize the Confederacy during the more recent Civil War had not entirely passed from the consciousness of either nation. Yet, by the end of the Wild West's run, Cody was being lauded by the *London Times* for doing his part in bringing "England and America" together.[6] The most striking occurrence of the run was Queen Victoria's visit to the show on May 11, 1887, , which marked her first public appearance since the death of her consort, Prince Albert, from typhoid fever on December 14, 1861. This and the subsequent command performance given at Windsor on June 20, 1887, are evidence of the extent to which Cody was, in addition to being a man of his own times, very much a "Renaissance man" out of his time—multi-talented and with a thirst for the patronage of the great and good that was, quite literally, food and drink to the great talents of fifteenth- and sixteenth-century Europe.

Cody is said to have remarked, when the Kings of Denmark, Belgium, Greece and Saxony and the Prince of Wales all rode in the Deadwood Stagecoach, "I've held four kings, but four kings and the Prince of Wales makes a Royal Flush such as no man ever held before."[7] His comment inscribes new meanings to such patronage, however, in an intercultural nexus that juxtaposes the contemporary and quintessentially American game of poker with the presence of personages from ancient royal houses of Europe. Cody, the nineteenth-century entrepreneur, was not slow to cash in on this winning hand, and he quickly had lithographs produced that depicted his head encircled by those of his royal patrons. These lithographs were soon reproduced as prints that subsequently became the basis for publicity posters. Indeed, publicity was food and drink to the "mobile dream factory [. . . . . .] producing narratives of heroic conquest for mass audiences"[8] that was Buffalo Bill's Wild West.

At the close of the American Exhibition, the show moved on to Birmingham and Manchester for shorter, although similarly successful, runs. It did so well that the following year the show remained in the north of England, appearing in Manchester again and also in Hull.

When the show opened in Paris on May 14, 1889, as part

of the Universal Exhibition, ten thousand spectators gave it an enthusiastic reception, and the "Marseillaise" was played after the "Star-Spangled Banner." In the absence of royalty, Monsieur Carnot, president of the French Republic, was the leading patron, and although the exiled Queen Isabel II of Spain attended a performance, the difference of emphasis in the French show reflected Cody and his troupe's understanding that Europe was not just one homogeneous setting for the reception of the accomplished product of American mass culture that the Wild West had become.[9]

Audiences in Paris were themselves culturally and linguistically diverse, reflecting not only the cosmopolitan nature of the city but also the fact that trains from various parts of the continent were bringing eager spectators from all over Europe to see the recently inaugurated Eiffel Tower, the industrial advances on show at the Exhibition, the Pavilions of the participating nations, the anthropological exhibition on human evolution, and, of course, Buffalo Bill and company. The clamor for tickets excited interest in the prospect of a more wide-ranging European tour, which the troupe undertook later that year and into 1890, travelling first to Lyons and Marseille in the south of France and then on to Spain, where they made a single five-week stop in Barcelona before proceeding through Italy, the Austro-Hungarian Empire, and Germany.

Wherever they stopped contemporary newspaper accounts not only spoke of the show's success but also provided evidence of the intercultural dialogue and exchange that was going on, with elements of the show being appropriated for various local purposes and to reflect local concerns. The show was parodied in London, Paris and Barcelona, and the French press used the figure of Cody to ridicule General Georges Boulanger.[10] The Catalan satirical magazine *Esquella de la Torraxa* even lampooned Francesc Rius i Taulet, the recently deposed mayor of Barcelona, by caricaturing him in a blanket and feathers begging for a job with the Wild West.[11] Louis Warren has rightly observed that "Europeans did not admire his [Cody's] show simply because they liked Americans. Buffalo Bill's Wild West drew huge crowds in the United Kingdom and on the Continent because of the ways that it spoke to European desires and anxieties."[12]

The 1891 season began in Germany and Belgium before the troupe returned to the British Isles where it was joined in April by twenty-three Lakota "prisoners of war" who had been released into Cody's custody less than three months after the so-called Ghost Dance uprising of the previous December. They provided a boost to the show's publicity by depicting the authentic savagery of the frontier as an imminent phenomenon, though the closest any of the prisoners ever came to actual rebellion was when they performed in Cody's interpretation of Indian-white relations in Scotland, England, and Wales.[13]

Spring 1892 saw a series of theatre appearances by an *ad hoc* concert party comprising the Cowboy Band, the Tyrolean Singers, and a group of twelve Indians who performed music, songs and, dances in a number of small venues around Glasgow.[14] The season culminated in another successful six-month stand in London, after which Buffalo Bill's Wild West would not be seen in Europe for almost a decade. The show that returned would be substantially different from that which had toured there before.

The intervening ten years were not kind to William F. Cody, the man who grew up with Manifest Destiny,[15] and whose life in many ways reflects the aspirations and disappointments of many Americans during the nineteenth century. With his rise from relative poverty to wealth, from obscurity to celebrity, Cody undoubtedly lived a version of the American dream, but he was also beset by the same boom- and-bust cycles that were known to homesteaders, factory workers and other circus owners and performers.

The circus industry was changing, as many small concerns folded under pressure from their larger rivals, while others were bought out by emerging super-companies like the Ringling Brothers and Barnum and Bailey.[16] The injection of cash that James A. Bailey's investment provided to the Wild West in the midst of one of Cody's many financial crises was effectively a buyout through which Bailey took a controlling interest at the request of Cody's partner Nate Salesbury. This had the positive side-effects of allowing the show to grow considerably and providing some measure of financial stability. It was only after Bailey's death in 1906, and in the wake of the financial controversies surrounding his will, that Cody's Wild West had to merge with Pawnee Bill's show in 1908.

In the second phase of its European activities the Wild West was bigger, and it incorporated a much more expansive sideshow operation. There would be few of the longer runs which had characterized the nineteenth-century version of the show. The standard operating procedure would now be a series of one night stands with only the occasional extended run in major cities where the market was projected to be sustainable. The progress of civilization that Cody had fictionalized and symbolized in the transformation of the West was being worked out in a very real sense in the transformation of the show itself. Improved infrastructure facilitated faster travel, technological advances made it possible to set up and dismantle more quickly, and the economic pressures that had put so many of the smaller troupes out of business had dictated the necessity to become part of a larger conglomerate. Clearly, the globalizing influences that would come to the fore throughout the twentieth century were already at work.

The turn of the century was also a difficult period in Cody's personal life. The loss of his acrimonious divorce case caused him to be roundly criticized in his hometown of North Platte, Nebraska, and lampooned in the national press. This negative publicity actually appears to have been damaging to him personally—to say nothing of the potential damage to his business interests—and Warren has described the years in Europe which followed as a "figurative exile that largely kept him from the public gaze in the United States."[17]

Exile or not, Cody was very much in the public gaze during the long and successful run in London through the second half of 1902 and the first three months of 1903. He spent the remainder of that year and the next traveling to numerous smaller venues across England, Scotland, and Wales. Press coverage of the show was almost universally positive, as the narrative of civilization's banishment of savagery from the globe continued to captivate audiences.[18] It was a discourse that clearly resonated with the late Victorian public of a British Empire on which the sun literally never set and which was just emerging from the Second Boer War, the latest of its own many colonial conflicts on its far-flung frontiers.

Charles Eldridge Griffin joined the show in Manchester in April 1903 and remained with it through the end of the 1906 season. He missed only the initial London run and the first few Manchester engagements during the four years in Europe to which his memoir refers. His work provides readers with an insider's view of the remaining dates in the British Isles, the year-long tour of France in 1905, complete with its iconography on the emerging *entente cordiale* with the United States, as well as the peripatetic 1906 season when the show ranged far and wide through Italy, the Austro-Hungarian Empire, Germany, Luxembourg, and Belgium, welcoming distinguished visitors from many royals houses along the way. Contemporary commentators, in Germany and Italy in particular, showed an increasing fascination with the Indians as romantic symbols of a preindustrial age.[19] Griffin's idiosyncratic commentaries, while often reflecting prevalent American views of the various European nations, stand in stark contrast to these German and Italian romantic ideals, both in the frankness of their tone and the down-to-earth realism of their content.

Griffin is generally positive about the English, who "respect and admire Americans more than the people of the States generally imagine,"[20] and the Germans, who "take every advantage of their natural resources,"[21] but his views on the French are more mixed. He comments favorably on their energy but condemns them for their "extreme excitability and social immorality."[22] Among Griffin's most poignant views are those on the ethnic diversity and linguistic mix of the cities the Wild West visited in the Austro-Hungarian Empire, a tinderbox only eight years before it would ignite Europe in four years of bloody war. He writes, "Some towns would be about equally divided between four or five nationalities, and, although they all understood German, the official language, each would insist on being addressed in his native language. We think we have a race problem in America, but it is more complicated and acute in Eastern Europe, and it is not a matter of color, either."[23]

Unless otherwise noted, all biographical details are based on Roger Grant's study, "An Iowan with Buffalo Bill: Charles Eldridge Griffin in Europe: 1903–1906," in *Palimpsest: Journal of the State Historical Society of Iowa* 54, no. 1 (January–February 1973): 2–14, which was based in part on material from interviews with Charles E. Griffin's nephew, John W. Griffin.

Notes

1. Griffin, *Four Years in Europe with Buffalo Bill*, 17.
2. Griffin, *Four Years in Europe with Buffalo Bill*, 18.
3. Griffin, *Four Years in Europe with Buffalo Bill*, 19, 95–96.
4. Blair, "Blackface Minstrels and *Buffalo Bill's Wild West*," 8.
5. Rydell and Kroes, *Buffalo Bill in Bologna*, 116.
6. *London Times*, November 1, 1887.
7. Russell, *Lives and Legends of Buffalo Bill*, 331.

8. Rydell and Kroes, *Buffalo Bill in Bologna*, 31.
9. Rydell and Kroes, *Buffalo Bill in Bologna*, 112.
10. Warren, *Buffalo Bill's America*, 349–50.
11. Marill Escudé, *Aquell hivern*, 105.
12. Warren, *Buffalo Bill's America*, 302.
13. Maddra, *Hostiles?*, 190.
14. Cunningham, "Your Fathers the Ghosts," 149–50.
15. Reddin, *Wild West Shows*, 54.
16. On which see in particular Assael, *The Circus and Victorian Society*.
17. Warren, *Buffalo Bill's America*, 524.
18. Warren, *Buffalo Bill's America*, 348.
19. On which see Fiorentino, "Those Red-Brick Faces," and Warren, *Buffalo Bill's America*, 345.
20. Griffin, *Four Years in Europe with Buffalo Bill*, 41.
21. Griffin, *Four Years in Europe with Buffalo Bill*, 81.
22. Griffin, *Four Years in Europe with Buffalo Bill*, 58.
23. Griffin, *Four Years in Europe with Buffalo Bill*, 79.

ABOUT THIS EDITION

By the end of his life William F. Cody had become the entertainment industry's first international celebrity, blazing a trail that was to be followed by others with the advent of mass communication media in the decades after his passing. The vehicle that brought him international stardom was Buffalo Bill's Wild West. During the three decades that he operated and appeared in various incarnations of "the western world's greatest travelling attraction,"[1] European and American audiences were offered a carefully crafted narrative of the history of geographic expansion in the trans-Mississippi west of the United States that displayed in itself the products of nineteenth- and early twentieth-century industrial civilization while purporting to represent authentically the savage life of the frontier.[2] From its inception in 1883, the show was a reflection of the dominant positivist ideology of progress from savagery to civilization seen through the lens of Cody's own imagination, with his own constructed persona at the heart of it all.

More than any other individual, it was Cody who brought America to the world, crafting out of his own biography, imagination, and ambition an international and intercultural legacy that is still debated by scholars nearly one hundred years on. Every year the museums dedicated to his memory—in Cody, Wyoming, Golden, Colorado, and North Platte, Nebraska—attract a steady stream of visitors from throughout the United States and abroad. Given the unquestioned international importance of Cody's life and works and the enduring interest they continue to engender, it is scarcely credible that the only contemporary book-length commentaries on his Wild West in Europe, which has been referenced by every leading Cody scholar from Don Russell to Warren,[3] has only ever appeared in one edition with a single print run of five hundred copies and that it is now only available to specialists in a small number of libraries and archives. And yet, though a century has passed since it first appeared, that is the case for *Four Years in Europe with Buffalo Bill*.

A number of writers, such as Robert Rydell and Rob Kroes, have linked the development of mass-market American cultural products in the late nineteenth century to the origins of American cultural imperialism, arguing that its emergence as a global phenomenon pre-dates the decades between the two world wars that had previously been generally accepted.[4] Others scholars, such as Warren, have identified the need for further study of "the show's meaning for its diverse European audiences."[5] It is in the context of these recent debates that this new edition of Griffin's memoir is presented: a first-person narrative in straightforward prose that forms part of the documentary record of William F. Cody's life and career. It sheds light on some of the deepest questions about nationalism, imperialism, and an emerging global mass culture that dominate contemporary scholarly and public interest by describing and commenting upon some of the key events of the Wild West's extensive European tours of 1902 to 1906.

It is not, however, the intention of this edition to be overly academic, for to do so would be a tremendous disservice to the original. Griffin's distinctive voice draws his readers in as he addresses them directly in an unselfconscious manner that is at no time dry or scholarly. In producing this authoritative version of his text, complete with the accompanying line drawings and photographs from the *princeps*, care has been taken to ensure the integrity of the original. Corrections have been made to some aberrant spellings, especially of foreign words and place names; a number of abbreviations in the original have been clarified in full words to make the text either more accessible (particularly when these refer to foreign currencies or measurements) or more consistent (such as in the names of months). The text is otherwise as it appears in the Stage Publishing Company edition of 1908. Where place names have subsequently been changed, the text has not been amended and the current place name is given in the notes.

These annotations serve to provide further information on some of the personalities mentioned, to contextualize the narrative within the scope of the scholarly discussions mentioned above, and to indicate those aspects of the 1902–1906 tours on which further published material is available (further source are listed in the bibliography).

As an appendix to the volume, a complete listing of the dates and venues for the Wild West tour's engagements is included. Based on the original route books, care has been taken to ensure that current place names and modern orthography are used throughout the appendix. Particular care has been taken in relation to the much changed map of central and eastern Europe in order to ensure that modern states that formed part of the Austro-Hungarian Empire have been correctly identified.

This new University of Nebraska Press edition of *Four Years in Europe with Buffalo Bill* will, therefore, make a key primary source more readily available for scholars engaging in these intercultural dialogues while offering Charles Griffin's own work to the more general audience that it has heretofore lacked. The edition has been produced as part of the print edition of The Papers of William F. Cody under the aegis of the project of the same name, located at the Buffalo Bill Historical Center in Cody, Wyoming.

Notes

1. Blair, "Blackface Minstrels and *Buffalo Bill's Wild West*," 3.
2. Sears, "Bierstadt, Buffalo Bill, and the Wild West in Europe," 3.
3. See Russell, *Lives and Legends of Buffalo Bill*, and Warren, *Buffalo Bill's America*.
4. Rydell and Kroes, *Buffalo Bill in Bologna*.
5. Warren, *Buffalo Bill's America*, 302.

1. James Bailey and "Buffalo Bill" Cody in about 1901.

2. Wild West advertising poster containing the images of female royal personages.

3. Wild West advertising poster containing the images of male royal personages.

4. Entente Cordiale poster from the 1904 French tour.

Four Years in Europe with Buffalo Bill

Four Years in Europe with Buffalo Bill

BY CHARLES ELDRIDGE GRIFFIN

A Descriptive Narrative of the
Big American Show's Successful Tour
in Foreign Lands,
Illustrated with Original Photos
by the Author.

TABLE OF CONTENTS

Buffalo Bill—A Sketch 5
James Anthony Bailey 13
Foreword 17

CHAPTER I. 1903
    Our ocean voyage—General impressions of Old
    England. 21

CHAPTER II. Summer 1903
    Opening of the season—Accident to Buffalo Bill. ... 27

CHAPTER III. Winter 1903–1904
    Wintering in London—Sights and scenes of the
    great city—A trip to "Gay Paree," the fashion
    capital of the world. 35

CHAPTER IV. 1904
    Second year of Buffalo Bill in Great Britain—A visit
    to the potteries—Bonnie Scotland 51

CHAPTER V. Winter 1904–1905
    Again in London—Shop showing—The Waverly
    carnival—Studying French 57

CHAPTER VI. 1905
    Grand opening at Paris—A zigzag tour of
    France—Disease among the horses—Tragedie
    des Cheveaux 69

CHAPTER VII. Winter 1905–1906
    Marseille, the gateway to the Orient—Wintering under canvas—More observations of French manners and customs 93

CHAPTER VIII. 1906
    Opening of the season at Marseille—Tour of Italy, Austria-Hungary, Germany and Belgium 103

CHAPTER IX. 1906–1907
    Closing of the tour—Departure for and arrival at New York—Impressions of New York after four years abroad 123

Official Roster of Buffalo Bill's Wild West
    Season 1907 127

Programme, Buffalo Bill's Wild West Season 1907 131

BUFFALO BILL—A SKETCH[1]

Although Colonel William F. Cody (Buffalo Bill) has a vast army of personal friends, his tremendous successes (yes, I meant that to be plural) have made him many envious enemies, who assiduously exaggerate and circulate all kinds of villainous and scurrilous stories about the great scout—but that is one of the penalties of being great and famous.

It is really too bad that everybody cannot know the Colonel as his friends know him. He is truly one of the best fellows in the world—open hearted and generous to a fault. Why, his managers have to hedge him in and keep the people from him during the season, otherwise he would have his tents filled with free tickets, and that would not do, as it takes an enormous pile of money to keep so vast a concern moving from day to day.

He is not such an old man as people generally imagine, either. It is common to hear them say, "Why, this cannot be Buffalo Bill—I heard of him when I was

---

1. Griffin's admiration of Cody—a sentiment not uncommon in the writings of those who worked closely with the showman—is clearly reflected in this sketch, as it is elsewhere in Griffin's memoir.

a boy." Doubtless that is true, as Buffalo Bill began making history when he was a boy fourteen years old, in Kansas, during the "Jayhawk" War.

William F. Cody (Buffalo Bill) was born in Scott County, Iowa, February 26, 1846. He moved to Kansas, with the rest of the family, when but eight years of age. His father was assassinated by the "Cesesh," in 1855.[2] He is a well preserved man of sixty-two years, and as he is temperate in all things except work, I should say, barring accidents, he is good for twenty-five years yet.

When the Grand Duke Frederick[3] met the Colonel at Vienna, in 1906, he said:

"How old are you, Bill?"

"Sixty."

"Is that all! Why, you are quite a boy yet."

The duke was then eighty-two years old, and it had been seventeen years since he had met Cody.

---

2. Griffin's reference to the death of Isaac Cody is inaccurate. Cody himself places the event in April 1857 (see *Life of Hon. William F. Cody, Known as Buffalo Bill*, 57) and identifies the cause as "liver disease," although he qualified the statement with the comment that Isaac had never fully recovered from the 1855 wound he received in the Kansas border disputes, which Griffin refers to as the "Jayhawk War."

3. Archduke Frederick Maria Albrecht, Duke of Teschen, was only fifty years old at the time of his meeting with Cody in 1906.

6   *FOUR YEARS IN EUROPE WITH BUFFALO BILL*

5. Pholtograph of Cody autographed and addressed to Charles Griffin, "In memory of four years in Europe."

6. Facsimile of letter from William F. Cody to Charles E. Griffin, dated January 7, 1908. It reads: "My Dear Griffin, Thanks your letter. Certainly you can use the photo for your book. Are you to be with us the coming season I hope so. I haven't had much rest this season winter I mean. As I have so much to do out here but it's a change from the show life. And I like to be kept busy and am feeling fine. Yours truly, W. F. Cody."

7. Photographs of Fred Martin (*top*) and George Sanger.

FAC SIMILE OF LETTER FROM LORD GEORGE SANGER, THE BRITISH BARNUM.

> Park Farm,
> East Finchley,
> London, N.W., Eng.
>
> Dear Mr. Griffin,
>   I am in receipt of your letter, and have the pleasure to enclose a photograph for insertion in your book, as requested.
>   Yours very truly,
>   George Sanger.
>
> C. E. Griffin, Esq.

8. Facsimile of George Sanger letter to Charles E. Griffin. "I am in receipt of your letter, and have the pleasure to enclose a photograph for insertion in your book as requested. Yours very truly, George Sanger."

9. Charles Eldridge Griffin.

JAMES ANTHONY BAILEY

The subject of this sketch was born at Detroit, Michigan, July 4, 1847, of Scotch-Irish parentage.[4] He left home at ten years of age, and for a time worked on a farm at $3.50 per month.

While serving as a bell-boy in a hotel at Pontiac, Michigan, Fred Bailey, general agent of the Lake & Robinson Circus, came there and engaged young Bailey to assist him.

This was his opportunity, and he took advantage of it. His rise from billposter to general agent was rapid, and finally a proprietor in 1872, when he entered into partnership with J. E. Cooper, forming the celebrated "Cooper & Bailey Great International Allied Shows," visiting Australia, New Zealand, South America and India, returning to America in 1878 and consolidating with Howe's Great London Shows.

4. Born James Anthony McGuiness, James A. Bailey rose through the ranks of the circus world from teenage runaway to successful owner and manager—along with P. T. Barnum—of the so-called Greatest Show on Earth. On the involvement of Barnum and Bailey with Cody's partner, Nate Salisbury, and the circumstances by which Bailey came to be a partner and co-owner of the Wild West Show, see in particular Russell, *Lives and Legends of Buffalo Bill*, 378–82; Kasson, *Buffalo Bill's Wild West*, 144–51; Bridger, *Buffalo Bill and Sitting Bull*, 408–10; and Carter, *Buffalo Bill Cody*, 380–81.

10. James Anthony Bailey.

In 1880 he forced P. T. Barnum into a partnership, forming the "Barnum & Bailey Greatest Show on Earth," which, with the exception of one year, he continued to manage up to the time of his death.

"The little Napoleon of show business"—what an apt synonym! What Napoleon was to the military world, James A. Bailey was to the circus business.

When Bailey picked up a newspaper he did not first turn to the baseball score, nor did he stop to read the news of the day until he had first scanned the market reports and ascertained the price of cattle, hogs, flour, potatoes, cotton, tobacco, butter, eggs, etc. That told him more than the most thrilling headline—that was his barometer to business conditions.

It was Bailey's master mind which conceived and executed the idea of making the Buffalo Bill Show a one-day stand show. The Wild West was so tremendously cumbersome that Colonel Cody himself never dreamed that it was possible to make one day stands with it, and for years it would take them two or three days to move from place to place, and would consequently make long stands at expositions and large cities.

In 1904 he invited the five Ringling brothers into partnership with him by selling them a half interest in the Forepaugh-Sells Show, probably seeing in them his only possible successors.

He was united in wedlock to Ruth L. McCaddon, of Zanesville, Ohio, who was his constant companion in all his struggles and triumphs, and the great showman paid a touching tribute to her devotion in his will. "I know of no one more entitled to the results of our combined labors than my beloved wife, Ruth L. Bailey." And all his vast estate, amounting to millions, was left to Mrs. Bailey, she being named as administratrix, without bond.

Mr. Bailey passed to the "great beyond" at his beautiful mansion at Mount. Vernon, New York, Wednesday afternoon, April 11, 1906, erysipelas being the cause of death. He was interred at Woodlawn Cemetery on Saturday, April 14.

Requiescat in Pace.

FOREWORD

When the late James A. Bailey, undisputed king of the show world, visited the Ringling Bros.' Circus, at Canton, Ohio, in June, 1902, he unconsciously, perhaps, paid the Ringling brothers the greatest compliment that could be paid to a rival concern, inasmuch as he had never before deigned to visit a similar institution personally. However, he would keep himself thoroughly posted in their movements by means of his many agents.

On this occasion several employees of the Ringling Show were approached in regard to a tour of England with Buffalo Bill's Wild West, the following Spring.

I was among the lucky ones, and when I received my contract I felt highly elated at the prospect of a European tour with the most successful amusement institution of modern times.

The great show was transported across the Atlantic on the S. S. St. Paul, American Line, in December, 1902.

A preliminary engagement was played at Olympia, London, opening on the afternoon of December 26, 1902 (Boxing Day), and continuing until April 4,

1903—one hundred and seventy-two performances being given in that city.[5] The show met with instant and long continued success.

It was visited twice by King Edward, Queen Alexandra, the Prince and Princess of Wales, together with numerous other royal personages, but as the writer was not a party to this preliminary, or prologue, performance, I will confine myself to a description of the road tour only, nine days elapsing from the closing in London until the opening in Manchester.

It is not my intention to tire the reader with useless verbiage or dry statistics, such as the ordinary Circus Route Book affords, but to give a straightforward narrative of the many interesting places visited, and the *contretemps* met with in such a stupendous undertaking.

Of course, I found plenty to criticise abroad, because it was all so different from what I had seen at home, but I trust I have not been too severe, and I hope any of my foreign friends who feel aggrieved will pay a visit to America, where, I dare say, they will find an abundant field for retaliation.

All of which is respectfully submitted,
Charles Eldridge Griffin.
New York, December, 1906.

---

5. On the 1902–1903 London run, see Gallop, *Buffalo Bill's British Wild West*, 216–22.

NOTICE

Every reader of this book should know the true life story of "Buffalo Bill," contained in "The Last of the Great Scouts," by Colonel Cody's sister, Helen Cody Whetmore. This book is an ornament to any library, contains 244 pages, large, clear type, gold side and back stamp, copiously illustrated by Frederic Remington and E. W. Deming, and intensely interesting and thrilling throughout.

Sent post paid on receipt of $1.00 by
Stage Publishing Co.
Box 431, Albia, Iowa.

CHAPTER I—1903

Our Ocean Voyage—General Impressions of Old England

We left New York City, Saturday, March 28, 1903, at four p.m., on the good ship Etruria, Cunard Line, for Merrie England.

The Etruria is one of the staunchest, even though it is the senior, of this oldest of the Atlantic liners. She is 540 feet long and 51 feet wide.

Dinner, our first meal on board, was served at six o'clock, and everyone was there with a normal appetite—but, "Oh, what a difference in the morning!"

We were then well out to sea, and the boat was rolling to "beat the band."

A few old salts smiled and ate their breakfasts, but the majority seemed bent on feeding the fishes.

I remained in my berth all day Sunday, unable to get up or to eat a bite. Monday morning I ventured on deck and the fresh sea air did me good—in fact, from that day on I enjoyed the trip, and ate my regular six meals a day.

They gave us breakfast at eight, bouillon and sandwiches at eleven, luncheon at twelve, tea at five, dinner at six, and supper at eight o'clock.

The first cabin or saloon is "gilt-edge," second

cabin good enough for anyone who does not want silk jackets on their potatoes or gold nails in their coffins, and third class, or steerage, is not at all bad going over, but they say it is something awful coming this way.

There was something new every day to vary the monotony. The first thing I would look for when I went on deck was three sea-gulls that followed us all the way over. One of the sailors told me that they would roost on the waves and sometimes on the ship at night.

One day we saw a whale spouting in the distance, and at another time we encountered a number of monster icebergs from the frozen North.

Impromptu concerts were given in the cabin each evening, which culminated in one grand affair April 3, at which time I had the honor of being made chairman of the evening. On April 4 another entertainment was given in the grand saloon for the benefit of the Seamen's Charity Fund, at which time the Rt. Hon. the Earl of Rosslyn[1] was made chairman. This is the earl who, it is said, came to America in search of an heiress, finally found one at Pittsburg and was "turned down" at the finish. He impressed me as being rather a brilliant young fellow, and not at all like the newspapers have made him appear.

A daily paper was issued on board, giving the news of the world by wireless telegraphy. They played quoits

---

1. James Francis "Harry" St. Clair-Erskine became the Fifth Earl of Rosslyn in 1890 at age twenty-one, on the death of his father, the Fourth Earl, Robert Francis St. Clair-Erskine, a prominent Scottish Conservative politician. The son held the title until his death in 1939.

11. *It was fun to watch the seagulls dive for biscuits which we would throw into the sea.*

on deck, had a billiard, card and bar room, and a well stocked library, so you see we were not badly treated at all.

After being out six days we sighted land—the rocky West coast of Ireland—and here our three sea-gulls were joined by thousands of others, thus losing their identity. It was interesting sport to throw crackers into the sea and watch the gulls dive for them.

The ship did not land at Queenstown,[2] but came to anchor, while harbor boats took off the mail and passengers. This was about one o'clock p.m. A number of real Irish lassies came aboard to sell their beautiful hand-made laces. It was a cold, rainy day, and it struck

2. The port of Cobh in the southwest of County Cork, Ireland, was known as Queenstown from 1849 to 1922, in commemoration of a visit by Queen Victoria.

12. All going out, nothing coming in.

me as peculiar that they should wear furs and straw hats, but I became accustomed to that incongruity after landing in England, as women wear straw hats there the year 'round.

Five o'clock Sunday morning we arrived at Liverpool. The machinery had stopped, the pulse of the big ship had ceased to beat, and everyone awoke with a start.

During the seven days consumed in the voyage, we had become so accustomed to the constant vibration that when it ceased, it put our nerves all on edge, as it were, and from that time until we landed, at ten a.m., all was bustle and excitement among the five hundred passengers.

As we scattered, many sad farewells were spoken, as sincere friendships and firm attachments are formed on an ocean voyage.

We had no trouble in passing through the customs, as England is a free trade country; tobacco, liquor and playing cards being about the only contraband articles of any consequence.

From Liverpool we took train at once for Manchester, and such funny little cars, they seemed to be no larger than our narrow gauge cars. There are first, second and third class cars, divided into compartments, with room for ten people in each compartment. The cars are not heated, but, on a cold day, they give you a foot warmer in the shape of a tank of hot water, which, if you go far, will be ice at the end of your journey. Neither are there any toilet conveniences, except on the long distance express trains. Another peculiarity of English railway travel is they do not check your baggage or luggage; you give a railway porter a penny or two to put your luggage on the train, and at your destination another porter takes care of it for a like amount. The rails are called "metals," the engineer a "driver," and the conductor a "guard."

Manchester is the second largest city in Great Britain,[3] being next to London in size. It is in Lancashire, the centre of the cotton spinning industry. They speak a very peculiar dialect, and it took us some time to get "next" to it. They have an excellent system of trolley cars or tramways, superior to any I have seen in the States. The cars or carriages are double deck, each car is licensed to carry just so many passengers, and are owned by the city.

3. According to the 1901 census, the population of Manchester was 543,872, making it the second largest city in England at the time. Glasgow, with a population in excess of 760,000, was the second largest city in Great Britain.

FOUR YEARS IN EUROPE WITH BUFFALO BILL 25

The English system of coinage is quite different from ours, the unit of value being pounds, shillings and pence. Twelve pence, one shilling; twenty shillings, one pound—($4.80 in our money). Paper money does not circulate promiscuously. A fellow might as well be broke as to be in London with a £5 note (about $25.00), as no one will take it unless endorsed by some well known business man or firm.

The Spring was very backward, and we all suffered with the cold, although the thermometer did not indicate cold weather. But the dampness was fierce. They use open fireplaces instead of stoves, and put on coal by the thimbleful.

I happened to be in the mill district one evening at six o'clock, and of all the noises I ever heard, the clatter of the wooden clogs on the pavement "took the biscuit." I can only liken it to a troupe of cavalry on the march.

The hotels, or "pubs," as they are called, are open Sunday, but restaurants and eating-houses are closed. So there is no trouble about getting plenty to drink, but I found it very difficult for a stranger to get anything to eat on a Sunday, even at such an important place as Liverpool.

I did not see a frame building or shingle roof in England, all being substantial brick or stone structures, with slate roofs.

Most of the buildings are from two to four stories. I did not see a "sky-scraper" in all Europe, there being a law forbidding the building of a house taller than the width of the street.

CHAPTER II—SUMMER 1903

Opening of the Season—Accident to Buffalo Bill

We opened the tenting season of 1903 at Brook's Bar, Manchester, April 13, Bankers' Holiday, to turn away business, in a cold drizzling rain, which turned to snow. At the opening performance Colonel Cody was thrown from his horse, or, rather, the horse stumbled,[1] severely spraining one of the Colonel's ankles, consequently he was unable to ride during the three weeks' engagement at Manchester, but was driven around the arena in a carriage at each performance.

Saturday, April 24, our press contingent was entertained by the Manchester Press Club, and I had the honor of closing the programme with an exhibition of Yankee magic. Lew Parker,[2] manager of privileges, arranged the programme, which was a most enjoyable one. Major John M. Burke, Harvey Watkins, Charles S. Wells and Dexter Fellows constituted our press

---

1. According to the *New York Times* of April 14, 1903, while rearing up, Cody's horse overbalanced and fell on him, causing the injury to his ankle.

2. Lew Parker was a veteran minstrel show performer, manager, and publicity agent who had been involved with Cody's Wild West since its earliest days. Parker published his own reminiscences in an undated (1910?) volume that includes some interesting reflections on the Wild West's earlier European tours. Griffin wrongly identifies him as "Lew Graham" in the original 1908 text.

staff, and a capable quartet they proved to be, judging from the immense amount of free advertising the show received.[3]

All the members of the English press I met were a fine lot of gentlemen, and decidedly friendly to Americans.

We closed our three weeks' stay at Manchester, Saturday night, May 2, and began a three weeks' engagement at Liverpool, Monday, May 4.

Sunday afternoon, May 10, the good Bishop of Liverpool held services in the arena for the benefit of the Wild West. Dr. Chavasse[4] is a grand, good man, and he delivered a beautiful sermon, which was highly appreciated by Colonel Cody and his motley assemblage of Indians, cowboys and rough riders from all nations. His lordship was assisted by a large choir of gentlemen and boys, the hymns sung being "Rock of Ages," "Oh, God, Our Help in Ages Past," and "Onward, Christian Soldiers."

The Bishop commenced his remarks by saying:

3. "Major" "Arizona" John M. Burke was another longtime associate of Cody who acted as press agent and advance agent for the Wild West on many occasions, including the European tours. Burke is sometimes suggested as the ghostwriter of material published in Cody's name. Harvey L. Watkins had acted as press agent on Barnum and Bailey's 1897 tour of Europe and authored a memoir of that tour published in the same year. According to Tom Cunningham, Charles S. Wells was the press agent who often acted as advance agent on the 1902–1906 tour. Cunningham, *"Your Fathers the Ghosts,"* 267. Dexter W. Fellows joined the Wild West as a press agent and went on to work in a similar capacity with the Ringling Brothers and Barnum and Bailey circuses. For more on his involvement with each see his autobiography, *This Way to the Big Show* (1936).

4. Dr. Francis James Chavasse was the Anglican Bishop of Liverpool from 1900 to 1923. Alan Gallop gives the account of the service that was published by the *Liverpool Daily Post* on May 11, 1903. Gallop, *Buffalo Bill's British Wild West*, 229.

"Colonel Cody and My Friends—It is a singular honor and pleasure my being here to speak to you as an Englishman. Between England and the United States of America I trust there will be never anything else but peace, for we worship God in the same faith and in the same language, and as a Bishop of the National Church, I came here to speak to you a few words on behalf of our Master, Christ."

His lordship then proceeded to address us on the words of the patriarch Job: "Behold, God is mighty and despiseth not anything."

During our second week at Liverpool, beginning May 11, we had the "Lord" George Sanger Show as opposition. This is the leading tented aggregation of all Europe, and corresponds in size with one of our ten-centers. Personally "Lord" George is a fine old gentleman of seventy-eight years, but looks twenty years younger.

Diamond and Beatrice, Prof. Roethig, the Royal Shanghai Chinese Troupe, and your humble servant, appeared at a smoker for the Liverpool Press Club, May 15.

At Birmingham, June 7, there was born to Chief Standing Bear and wife Laura (Sioux), a squaw[5] papoose, the only one ever born in Great Britain.[6] The little stranger was duly christened Alexandra-Pearl-

---

5. Many people, particularly among American Indian communities, now find the use of this term profoundly offensive. There is no indication that it was considered to be so in Griffin's day and its use is maintained here with sincere apologies to readers who may find the term offensive.

6. An Indian child had been born with the Wild West in Europe before Red Shirt's wife gave birth to her child in Paris in 1889.

13. Frederick Bailey Hutchinson.

Olive-Octavia-Birmingham-England-Standing Bear.[7] Two hours after giving birth to the child the mother walked across a large field to our big dining pavilion, ate a hearty meal and returned to her *tepee* without assistance. Two days later Manager Parker had them on exhibition in the annex, where they proved a potent attraction.

During the Birmingham engagement Alfonso, our human ostrich, swallowed a £5 note for a skeptic who had more money than brains. Talk about "being from Missouri," you certainly have to show them over there.

I am sure the reader will pardon me for recording here a very pleasant affair, and especially so to myself, which occurred at Kidderminster, June 16, at which time I was presented by the attaches of the Wild West Side Shows with a handsome gold medal to commemorate my forty-fourth birthday.

June 17 Colonel Cody's valet suddenly disappeared with a lot of jewels, viz.: A diamond studded pin, given to Colonel Cody by King Edward VII, at Olympia; a double gold rope chain; a diamond horseshoe pendant, presented by the Wild West company; buffalo head cuff links, given by the Grand Duke Alexis of Russia,[8] and about £4 ($20.00) in gold coin.

7. Standing Bear's own account gives the baby's name as Alexandra Birmingham Cody Standing Bear. Standing Bear, *My People the Sioux*, 266.
8. The Grand Duke Alexei Alexandrovitch was the fourth son of Tsar Alexander II of Russia, who famously journeyed to the United States in 1872. Cody acted as a guide for him in a buffalo hunt on the Kansas plains and gives his account of the event in his autobiography. *The Life of Hon. William F. Cody* 295–305.

The matter was placed in the hands of C. C. Murphy, our special Pinkerton detective, who, after three days, captured the thief, recovered the jewels, and had the culprit sentenced to "gaol" (that's the way they spell it over there) for six months at hard "labour."

June 27 Jacob Posey, our efficient master of stock, was presented with a fine silver mounted cane by the members of the company, the occasion being "Popular Posey's" fortieth birthday.

We celebrated our national holiday, July 4, with a grand banquet at Aberdare, South Wales. The decorations were especially fine, and Colonel Cody made one of his characteristic speeches.

At Swansea, Wales, July 14, I was made F. O. S. and the Sloper award of merit presented to me. The Sloper Club[9] is a popular London organization.

The first fatal accident occurred at Bristol, July 23. Isadore Gonzalez, one of the Mexican riders, was thrown from his horse and instantly killed. He was buried at Bristol. It is just as well, perhaps, that the general public do not realize the danger that forever attends the participants of the Wild West performances. Every time they enter the arena, especially in the bucking horse act, they practically take their lives in their hands.

At Taunton, August 3, for the second time this season, we showed day and date with Lord George

9. The Sloper Club was a Victorian gentlemen's club, located in India Street, in central London.

Sanger's Circus. It being Bank Holiday, both shows did capacity business.

We showed at Hastings, August 20. This is one of the favorite seaside Summer resorts of Great Britain, and we were blessed with a beautiful day and corresponding business. Our camp was pitched facing the beach, which was about one hundred yards distant, and we enjoyed ourselves on the sands between shows. Our trains were left at St. Leonards, three miles distant, the drive being along a high sea wall. At night a fierce storm arose and some of the drivers were completely engulfed by the high waves dashing and breaking over the wall.

During the season of 1903 our tour was confined to England and Wales. We heard the clatter of the clogs in Lancashire, saw the noble Hereford on his native heath, ate Banbury cakes from the original cookshop at Banbury, and Yarmouth bloaters at Yarmouth.

The season closed at Burton-on-Trent October 23. Colonel Cody and the American contingent of the Wild West sailed October 24 from Liverpool per S. S. Etruria, Cunard Line, for America, to spend the Winter months at their various Western homes, while the paraphernalia, railway cars, wagons, horses, tents, etc., were taken into Winter quarters at Stoke-on-Trent. We had a very pleasant and prosperous season, notwithstanding the fact that the elements were against us most of the time. Three hundred and thirty-three performances were given, and it can be recorded with satisfaction that only one performance was omitted, at Bradford, evening of October 6,[10] and that made necessary as a matter of public safety on account of the high gale prevailing at the time.

The tour consisted of one hundred and ninety-four days, divided as follows: Two stands of three weeks; one, two weeks; two, one week; two, four days; three, three days; six, two days, and seventy-eight, one day.

Only seven parades were given during the entire season, and those mainly as competitive measures at points where some of the English circuses were exhibiting on the same day.

The weather conditions throughout the entire season were most depressing, and the fact is recorded by the English press that never in the history of the country has there been a Summer where climatic conditions were as bad as those of this year. The coldest day was at Manchester, April 16, when the thermometer registered 31 degrees, while the warmest was experienced at Hereford, July 2, when the mercury mounted to 86 degrees—quite a contrast to weather experienced by troupers in the States.

---

10. On the three performances which did take place in Bradford on October 5 and 6, 1903, see Noble, *Around the Coast with Buffalo Bill*, 111–12. The afternoon performance of the second day went ahead in a downpour of rain but the evening performance was canceled due to concerns for public safety when the wind strength increased.

CHAPTER III—WINTER 1903–1904

*Wintering in London—Sights and Scenes of the Great City—
A Trip to "Gay Paree," the Fashion Capital of the World*

We left Burton, our closing stand, at eight-thirty a.m., October 24, by the Midland Railway, and arrived at St. Pancras Station, London, at twelve-thirty, noon.

Having considerable heavy luggage, we experienced some difficulty in getting it transferred to King's Cross Station, Metropolitan underground railway, as baggage wagons are not waiting for you, like birds of prey, in the States, such work being done by "outside porters," with push carts. While it would have cost at least $2.00 to have our luggage transferred in New York, it only cost a half crown (62 cents) in London. However, every railway porter who handles your luggage expects a tip—in fact, the tipping system is so much in vogue that all public servants, to use a "flash" expression, "have their mitts out." Waiters in first class hotels and restaurants receive no wages at all. On the contrary, they usually pay for the privilege of working by dividing their tips with their chief or head waiter.

The service of the Metropolitan underground railway is not so good as the Boston subway. Soft coal is used, which makes it very dirty, and the cars are old fashioned, but there is no overcrowding, and I believe they can handle more people in a given length of time than we can by our system. There are no surface tramways in London proper, the Metropolitan covering practically the entire business section with an inner and outer circle.

The "tuppenny tube," Yerkes' new system,[1] running from Shepherd's Bush, West London, through Central London, to the Bank of England, is up-to-date, and even ahead of the Boston subway. Electricity is used for motive power, and the cars are built on the American plan.

Large double-deck 'buses or stages, drawn by two horses (they have since been almost entirely superseded by motor 'buses), take care of the passenger traffic on the surface in Central London. The top of the 'bus is a good vantage ground from which to view the sights of the city.

I felt more at home in London than in any part of England.

There are American shoe stores, American quick lunches, American pharmacies, American barbers, American dentists, American bars, American this and American that, with the irrepressible American himself on every hand "blowing his horn," and his money at the same time—a verification of the immortal Lincoln's words, "He who bloweth not his own horn verily it shall not be blown."

---

1. On Charles Tyson Yerkes, a controversial Philadelphian financier who came to London from his Chicago base in 1900 with the backing of considerable American investment and played a leading role in the development of the London underground system in the opening years of the twentieth-century, see Franch, *Robber Baron*.

14. Paris office and advance staff.

After getting comfortably settled in a flat in the West End of London I started out to see the city. I asked a "bobby" which 'bus for Piccadilly Circus? He said: "You'll see the name on the 'bus." Then I commenced reading the signs on the 'buses as they hove in sight: "Grape Nuts," "Fry's Cocoa," "Mellin's Food," "Pear's Soap," "Carter's Little Liver Pills," etc. Finally, when a 'bus was a block past, I discovered in the least conspicuous place in small letters, "Piccadilly Circus." At last I got the right 'bus, but when we got to Piccadilly Circus there was no circus there. Here in "Ole Lunnon" they have a fashion of calling a circle or centre, from which several streets radiate, a circus, hence Piccadilly Circus, Ludgate Circus, Oxford Circus, etc.

15. George Starr (*top*) and Jule Keene.

It will not be surprising to those who know me to learn that the first place of amusement I visited in London was Maskelyne & Cook's Egyptian Hall, of thirty years' standing, in Piccadilly. They presented a refined entertainment of magic and mystery. The feature of the programme was Herr Valladon, the clever magician, who afterwards toured this country with our great and only Kellar, creating a most favorable impression. The hall itself is small, seats perhaps five hundred people, odd and curious, suggestive of mystery—looks as though it might be a vault in one of the ancient Pyramids. It was in this hall that P. T. Barnum first exhibited General Tom Thumb to London, and where Artemus Ward[2] showed his "Grate Morril Paneramy."

Other places of interest I visited on this occasion were the Art Gallery in Trafalgar Square, the Houses of Parliament, Hotel Cecil, Mansion House, where the Lord Mayor holds forth; Tower of London, Bank of England, in Threadneedle Street; St. Paul's Cathedral, etc., all of which, on account of their antiquity, reminds one of the grandeur of ages past. I will give detailed descriptions of most of these places when I have more leisure to visit them.

One Sunday morning, chaperoned by a Hebrew friend, I visited the famous "Petticoat Lane," in Whitechapel, where the Jews' Saturday market is held.

2. Artemus Ward was the *nom de plume* of the American satirical writer and lecturer Charles Farrar Brown, who traveled to England in 1866 and exhibited the *Great Moral Panorama* (parodied here with Griffin's idiosyncratic spelling).

There are miles of narrow streets, with squalid shops and booths on both sides of the curb, with every conceivable thing on sale, from fine bric-a-brac to bologna sausage and winkles (a snail-like shell food, very popular among the poor class). The streets are packed with all classes of humanity. Here you get some idea of the immensity of London.

They have a peculiar system of auctioneering. For example, an article is started at a high figure and the price lowered until a buyer is found.

Imagine, if you can, the combined population of Iowa, Minnesota, Dakota and Nebraska confined to one of our good sized counties, and you have some idea of the density of the population of London, which, in reality, is a country in itself—more interesting than any country I have ever visited.

I left London Saturday, December 12, for a four weeks' engagement at Bostock's Hippodrome,[3] Paris, which was in gala attire for *la fete de Noel* (Christmas holidays). The boulevards were lined with booths for the sale of holiday goods, and the numerous portable "show shops" were erected at the intersection of principal thoroughfares, giving it the appearance of a great street fair.

Shortly after my arrival in Paris the morning papers

3. Englishman Frank C. Bostock started his career in small circuses around the English Midlands and went on to travel the world, surviving attacks by lions and tigers, to exhibit in cities such as Paris, Indianapolis, and New York, ultimately becoming the foremost animal trainer of his day. Bostock's volume on the training of wild animals has remained in print almost continuously since its first publication in 1902, most recently reissued in 2003.

came out with a "scare head," *"Paris Sans Pain"* (Paris without bread). A big *boulangers'* (bakers') strike was on, and troops of cavalry paraded the streets to prevent rioting.[4]

They bake loaves of bread in Paris fully a yard in length, cut off as much as you wish and sell it by the *kilo* (two pounds, our weight, making one *kilo*).

Sunday is the last day of the week in Paris, and is a day set out for pleasure and recreation. I have been informed that there are thirty thousand Americans residing in Paris. It is a common saying in New York that all good Americans go to Paris when they die. It is therefore somewhat astonishing that the Franco-American population is not greater than it is.

The Hippodrome is located in the Boulevard de Clichy. Although one of the finest amusement temples in the world, it was a financial failure until the advent of Frank C. Bostock, an Anglo-American. The building is beautifully finished and furnished throughout; the arena is 125 feet by 250 feet, and the seating capacity is 9,000. Business was immense from the time of Mr. Bostock's opening, thousands being turned away Sundays and *fete* days.

Frank C. Bostock is a showman in the best and broadest sense of the word. I only wish the show world had more like him. Although born in the business, he was educated by his parents for the Church. At the age

---

4. The *New York Times* of December 23, 1903, makes no suggestion of rioting as the reason for the rigorous policing but rather the desire to prevent the bakers' strike from spreading to other food industries.

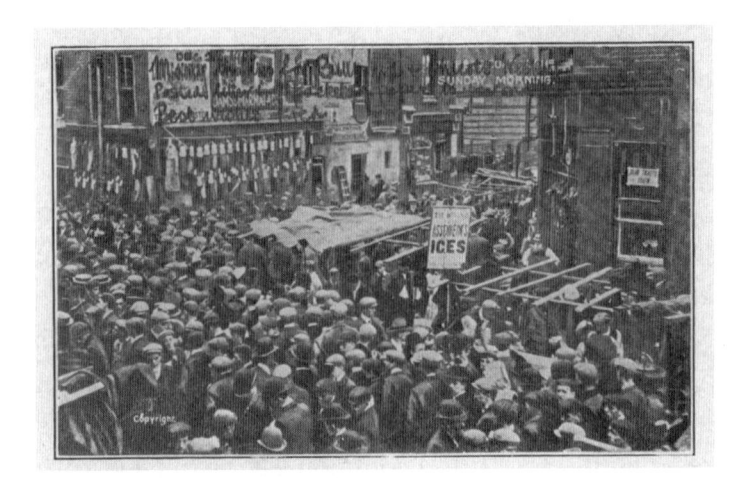

16. Petticoat Lane, London (*top*), and Bostock's Hippodrome, Paris.

of twenty-six he found old England, his native country, too small for his progressive ideas, and therefore, in 1892, he went to America for elbow room. Here he had room to expand, and after conquering the largest cities in the Western Hemisphere, it was but proper that he should "tackle" the effete East, and have the fashion capital of the world do him homage. Long live "Bostock, the Animal King!"

After a month's sojourn in the gay capital of France, I was glad to get back to London, where I could make my wants known without making signs. Some of those people who continually poke fun at and take advantage of foreigners (and there are plenty of them in every country) should visit a foreign land themselves and see how they like it. From what I saw of Paris I did not like it as well as London; and London—well, London is not New York.

I had begun to think that I was to be denied the privilege of seeing a London fog, but I was disillusioned Saturday morning, January 23, by waking up and finding it still dark at nine a.m. The papers declared it to be the worst fog of the century. The street lamps were burning all day, and even then you could not see two feet in front of you. It actually seemed as though you could cut it with a knife. My studio was in West Kensington, opposite the new Post Office Savings Bank Building, which is one of the largest structures in Great Britain, employing 3,000 government clerks of both sexes. The electric lights in this big building looked, through the fog, like stars glimmering through a cloudy sky. After paralyzing business for the day and causing many accidents, it disappeared as mysteriously as it came. No one seems to know where it comes from or where it goes to.

Talk about "Winter lingering in the lap of Spring." During the Summer of 1903 we had Winter all Summer, and, just to even things up, it seems, during the Winter of 1903–4 we had Summer all Winter; in fact, I did not see a snowflake, though there were some little flurries of snow in the midlands to the North of us. However, we did have an abundance of rain. The River Thames was four miles wide in places, and many farms were flooded. January was warmer than June of the preceding year. In February grass was green, butterflies were caught on the wing, and the half tame birds in the parks were nesting. Even the snakes at the Zoo had roused themselves from their dormancy and were shedding their skins. Of such are the vagaries of British weather, but there—an English gentleman told me once: "We do not have weather here; we only get samples from America."

In February, 1904, I paid a second visit to the Tower of London.[5] This ancient castle was founded by Caesar during the Roman occupation, and completed by William the Conqueror in 1078. It embraces almost every style of architecture that has flourished in England

---

5. Although built within the ancient walls of the Roman city which was to become London, there is no evidence for Griffin's fanciful claim that the Tower of London was started by Caesar. The earliest known construction work on the site was the fortress built by William the Conqueror in 1078.

since its inception, as the various rulers have added to and made alterations from time to time. It was originally built for a fortress, but has been used as the seat of government, the king's palace, an arsenal, and is now converted into a museum. The inner ward is reached by going over a stone bridge. Passing the Bell Tower and the King's House on the left, and the Traitor's Gate on the right, we then go under the Bloody Tower, turn to the right and we are at Wakefield Tower, where we inspect the crown jewels.

The king's crown, which occupies the most prominent position in the case, was made for the coronation of Queen Victoria, in 1838, from older crowns and the royal collection. There are a number of other crowns, viz: Those of Queen Alexandra, Queen Mary II, Charles II, Prince of Wales and Mary of Modena, second wife of James II.[6] The latter is said to be the oldest. It is needless to add that the various crowns contain many costly and historic jewels. Here also may be seen the royal plate, many jeweled swords and royal regalia of various kinds and epochs.

We will now retrace our steps, pass back under the Bloody Tower. To the left we pass, on a raised platform,

---

6. Queen Alexandra, the wife of King Edward VII, was the reigning monarch of the time. Queen Mary II reigned jointly with her husband, William III, from 1689 to 1702. King Charles II reigned from 1651 to 1685, although he was not officially recognized as king until the Restoration of the Monarchy in 1660, after the demise of Oliver Cromwell's Commonwealth. Mary of Modena was the Catholic second wife of James II of England (James VII of Scotland), who was king from 1685 until deposed by Parliament in 1688 amid fears that the birth of his son, also called James, might mark the return of a Catholic monarchy.

the gun carriage which carried the mortal remains of Queen Victoria to her last resting place at Frogmore. We next enter the Great White Tower, which is the most conspicuous part of the entire structure. We pass up a small flight of time-worn stone steps, through the Chapel of St. John, where many of the beheaded martyrs lie buried, into the Armory, which was formerly known as the Council Chamber and Banquet Hall. It is divided into four rooms—two upstairs and two down. These four large rooms are completely filled with arms and armor for both man and horse, representing all countries and all ages.

Leaving the White Tower, we pass over the spot, marked by a tablet, where Queen Anne Boleyn, Lady Jane Grey, the Earl of Essex, and various others, were executed, the block and axe still being on exhibition in the Armory.[7] Strangely enough, the benches which surround this sacred spot were occupied by solemn looking ravens, a sinister reminder of the tragedies that were here enacted centuries ago. The unhappy victims were all beheaded with an axe except Queen Anne Boleyn, who was decapitated with a sword.

7. Queen Anne Boleyn, the second wife of King Henry VIII, was executed in 1536 on charges of adultery, incest, and treason. Lady Jane Grey was the *de facto* Queen of England for nine days in July 1553 upon the death of her cousin, King Edward VI, who had named her as his Protestant successor in preference to his Catholic half-sister, Mary Tudor. When Parliament recognised Mary as queen, Lady Jane Grey was imprisoned in the Tower and convicted of high treason. She was executed in private the following year amid fears that the Protestant "Wyatt's Rebellion" would overthrow Mary and restore Jane to the throne. Robert Devreux, Second Earl of Essex, was a former favorite of Anne Boleyn's daughter, Queen Elizabeth I, but was executed on her orders in 1601 for his involvement in a failed attempt to overthrow the monarch.

The executioner of the Earl of Essex required three strokes of the axe to do his bloody work, and was in turn mobbed and beaten by the populace on his way home.

Next we visit the Beauchamp Tower, whose ancient prison walls are covered with inscriptions, carved in stone, in many instances by kings and queens. The history of these inscriptions alone make quite a large book. One over the fireplace, in Latin, is especially pathetic: "The more suffering for Christ in this world, the more glory with Christ in the next.—Arundell,[8] June 22, 1587." Taken all in all, the Tower of London is one of the most interesting relics of bygone ages in all Europe.

The Drury Lane pantomime is as much an English institution as a London fog or the income tax. Every playhouse of any consequence concentrates the efforts of the year on this holiday spectacle. The pantomime season begins on Boxing Night, December 26, and runs until the beginning of Lent. The various theatres will present "Puss in Boots," "Aladdin," "Cinderella," "Blue Beard," "The House That Jack Built," and so on through the entire gamut of fairy tales. I had the pleasure of attending the Theatre Royal, Drury Lane, seeing the time honored "Humpty Dumpty," with such notables in the cast as Dan Leno, the king's jester; Herbert Campbell (both of whom have since passed to the great beyond), Harry Randall, and many others equally as

8. The inscription is attributed to Philip Howard, Earl of Arundell, a staunch Catholic who was imprisoned in the Tower from 1584 until his death some ten years later.

clever, but not with the reputations.[9] Our definition of a pantomime is "a play without words." The English pantomime is therefore paradoxical, being pantomime that is not pantomime at all, but what we would call extravaganza or spectacular burlesque. Americans as a rule do not take to this style of entertainment, but I enjoyed it very much, although parts of it I found a little tedious. The comedy was good, being mainly topical, bristling with local hits, the singing fair, the ballets fine, and the scenery simply gorgeous.

That reminds me of an incident that happened in New York recently—pardon the digression: Young "Bob" Hunting, aged six, had been up to see the Barnum & Bailey Show at Madison Square Garden, and was describing to me what he had seen, with all the eloquence at his command. He had apparently got to the end of his string, so I asked him as seriously as I could: "Now, 'Bob,' what was the best thing you saw up there?" He studied for a moment and then answered enthusiastically: "Why, the wagons."

I think the English respect and admire Americans more than the people of the States generally imagine. Of course, we have our critics as well as our

9. Dan Leno, a stand up comedian, clog dancer, and noted pantomime dame, was the leading star of London music hall in the late nineteenth and early twentieth centuries. Herbert Campbell, another leading music hall performer, was famously partnered with Dan Leno in a comic double act at the Drury Lane Theatre, and became the forerunner of the many comic partnerships in twentieth-century music hall, vaudeville, and, later, cinema. Thomas William "Harry" Randall rose through the ranks of British music hall, beginning as a bottom of the bill comedic singer in the 1880s to become a versatile headline act touring throughout the British Isles in the early decades of the twentieth century. As with Dan Leno, Randall was famous as a pantomime dame.

champions. Englishmen who have made failures in the States are prone to condemn everything American, but, happily, they are few and far between. Some American artists (all performers are artists in Europe) who have never been considered "in it" at home, have achieved great success over here. On the other hand some famous stars at home have been dismal failures on this side. It is human nature to "speak well of the bridge that carries us safely over"—that is, from a selfish standpoint.

Although clothing and dress goods are somewhat cheaper in London than America, it cost us almost a third more to live there than in New York. I will quote some of the prices which prevailed while we were there: Flour, 20 cents for five pounds; bread 7½ cents for a pound loaf; milk, 7 cents per quart; potatoes, 2 cents per pound; tea, 42 cents per pound; coffee, 42 cents per pound; soft coal, 33 cents per hundredweight; butter, 30 cents per pound; margarine, 12 cents per pound; eggs, 20 cents and 30 cents per dozen; rump steak, 24 cents per pound; sirloin steak, 48 cents per pound; pork chops, 18 cents per pound; chickens, 60 cents and 80 cents each; mutton, 8 cents and 14 cents per pound. Well, I ate plenty of mutton, which reminds me:

> Mary had a little lamb,
>   It grew up into mutton;
> I ate so very much of it,
>   I feel just like a but'n.

CHAPTER IV—1904

*Second Year of Buffalo Bill in Great Britain—
A Visit to the Potteries—Bonnie Scotland*

I left the English metropolis to begin my second tour of Great Britain about the middle of April, beginning the season with Buffalo Bill's Wild West, at Stoke-on-Trent, Monday, April 25.

Mr. Lew Parker had during the Winter resigned as manager of privileges, and returned to the States to take the same department with Ringling Bros.' World's Greatest Shows, and I was selected by the management to fill his position with the Wild West.

Stoke is the centre of the potteries district, and the Winter quarters of Barnum & Bailey, Ltd.,[1] which forms a small city in itself.[2] There are twelve buildings of brick and iron, everything being under cover from railway cars to stakes and toe-pins. Here everything connected with the Wild West had been gone over,

---

1. Griffin's own note: In December, 1907, the Ringling Bros. acquired, by purchase, all the rights, titles and interests of the Barnum & Bailey, Ltd., which was an English syndicate. This makes the five Ringlings, viz., Al., Otto, John, Charlie and Alf. T., the most extensive owners of show property in the world-the Ringling Bros.' World's Greatest Shows, Barnum & Bailey's Greatest Show on Earth and the Adam Forepaugh & Sells Bros.' Combined Shows, comprising the three biggest shows in the world, excepting, of course, Buffalo Bill's Wild West.

2. On the Wild West in Stoke see Gallop, *Buffalo Bill's British Wild West*, 222–24.

repairs made where necessary, painted and renewed during the Winter months, a force of two hundred men being employed for this purpose.

This was my first visit to Stoke, and I found it very interesting. It reminded me of Johnstown, Pennsylvania, before the flood—a dingy conglomeration of villages under separate municipal control, embracing all together a dense population of working people, a veritable beehive of industry. Both coal and potter's clay is mined there in enormous quantities; in fact, the place is all undermined, and occasionally there is a cave-in, houses demolished, and lives lost, just the same as in the mining districts of America. I went on a tour through one of the big potteries, and I found the process of making an ordinary dinner plate both complex and interesting. China clay, when ready for the potter's wheel, is composed of rot marl (clay), granite, Cornwall stone, flint and feldspar, all ground fine and reduced to a putty-like substance, which is molded into shape on a revolving wooden wheel, dried and then baked in an immense kiln with graduated heat. The people of the potteries are hard-working, warm-hearted, bright, kind and intelligent.

After showing a week in the midlands we jumped over into North Wales, to the beautiful and picturesque Llandudno-by-the-Sea. We put in three weeks in Wales, from May 2 to 21, then into Cornwall to Land's End, showing at Penzance May 30. Thence Northeast, showing around and in the suburbs of London for three weeks. July 13 found us at Windsor,[3] and I had the pleasure of visiting historic Windsor Castle, over which floated the royal standard, denoting that King Edward was at home.

At York,[4] July 4, the whole show was a mass of red, white and blue bunting, in honor of our national holiday, the bands played patriotic airs, and the entire company sat down to a regular Yankee dinner, which almost made us forget, for the time being, that we were "strangers in a strange land."

July 11 to 16 our tents were pitched on the Town Moor Recreation Grounds, Newcastle-on-Tyne, the most beautiful park I have ever seen used for show purposes, abounding in beautiful lakes, fountains, islets, flowers, shrubbery and grassy lawns. Newcastle is one of the leading manufacturing cities of Great Britain, and is truly the metropolis of the North of England, full of historic interest and replete with the most modern phases of a manufacturing city. The great national arsenal and ordnance works, and numerous shipbuilding plants, among them the largest one in the world, are located between Newcastle and the sea.

July 26 the big Western Show made its entry into

3. Royal patronage was hugely important to the Wild West in Europe, as exemplified by the numerous references made by Griffin to visits to the show by royal patrons. On the appearance at Windsor and other royal visits to the show in England see Gallop, *Buffalo Bill's British Wild West*, 218, 220–22.

4. Noble, *Around the Coast with Buffalo Bill*, 107–24, discusses in detail the show's appearances around Yorkshire and Lincolnshire from September 23 to October 14, 1904, specifically the York appearance at 121–22.

Bonnie Scotland[5] at Hawick, pronounced by the natives, Hike, and we had a two mile "hike" to the show grounds through a Scotch mist, which in America we would call a drizzling rain. Here I saw the first thistle I had seen for more than two years, and it seemed like seeing some one from home, as we used to have more than a plenty of them in the old Hawkeye State where I was raised. There were 20,000 soldiers encamped at Hawick, including the king's favorite regiment, the famous Black Watch.

At Dumbarton, where we stopped for one day, July 30, our tents were pitched in another beautiful park, with all the trimmings—lakes, swans, etc., while Giant Ben Lomond, famous as the rendezvous of Rob Roy, loomed up in the distance.

August 1 to 6 found us at Glasgow, the metropolis of Scotland, and there we did the largest week's business in the history of the Wild West as a traveling organization, and only excelled by the abnormal business of the Chicago World's Fair season, in 1893.

Sunday morning, August 7, we invaded the Scottish capital, one of the grandest cities I have ever visited. Princes Street, with its rows of fine stores on one side, and a beautiful valley between the mountains, topped by historic Edinburgh Castle on the other side, is certainly a picturesque dream.

While Edinburgh is "in it" for beauty, it does not compare so favorably with Glasgow for business,

---

5. Making extensive use of local newspaper archives, Tom Cunningham provides a detailed account of the Scottish engagements on the tour. *"Your Fathers the Ghosts,"* 169–313.

notwithstanding our success was very pronounced. Municipally both cities are splendidly administered. We put in two months in Scotland, and our business was immense throughout the Scottish tour.

We re-entered England at Carlisle, September 15, and the remaining five weeks of the season were put in on the West coast of England, closing our season at Hanley, North Staffordshire, Friday, October 21. The next day, October 22, Colonel Cody and the Wild West contingent sailed for America, while the horses, rolling stock and paraphernalia went into Winter quarters at Stoke-on-Trent.

During the season we covered England, Scotland and Wales, from the East to the West, and Land's End on the South to John O'Groat's on the North. Considering that very few Englishmen have accomplished this, it is somewhat of an achievement to boast of. Press Agent Frank Small,[6] who wore his Scottish kilts on the Scotch tour, took photographs of the Indians at Land's End and John O'Groat's.

To the average foreigner it would perhaps seem incredible that such a vast concern as Buffalo Bill's Wild West, comprising 800 people and 500 horses, could put in two seasons, or more than twelve months' continuous showing, in such a small section of territory. While the tight little island, only a speck on the map of the world, is not so small as some Americans

6. "Colonel" Frank Small worked with the Wild West as a press agent for a number of years before moving on to work with other circuses and shows. Cunningham includes one of the Indian photographs to which Griffin refers. *"Your Fathers the Ghosts,"* 242–43.

imagine, considering the vast section of the earth's surface it has populated and dominated, it is very large indeed.

The season has been the best in the history of the show, and the members of the Wild West, from the highest to the lowest, bid farewell to merry old England with keen regrets and sincere good wishes for the prosperity of her hospitable people, the fairest and squarest country in the world to a stranger.

CHAPTER V—WINTER 1904–1905

Again in London—Shop Showing— The Waverley Carnival—Studying French

At the close of the season of 1904 I returned to my studio at West Kensington, London. By this time I was well acquainted in the big city and found it a first class place to live. During this time I had all kinds of experiences in show business, from "penny gaffs" to music halls and society entertainments—my adventures in that line will make a book of itself.

But I must tell you about my second visit to Scotland and the great Waverley Carnival. I left gray old London for Edinburgh, justly styled by tourists as the modern Athens, a distance of four hundred miles. The train runs through without change and is modern, being built as nearly on the American plan as it is possible to have them over there, with their short curves and narrow tunnels. They call them corridor trains. Sleeping and dining cars are run through. They serve an excellent four course luncheon for the low price of a half crown (sixty-two cents). Until recently there were three classes on all British railways, but a great many of them have abolished the second class, retaining only the first and third, which are practically the same, except in price—indeed, you would hardly know the difference but for the paper labels which are pasted on the doors of the compartments to denote the class, and these are changed as occasion requires. The advent of the American one class trolley cars and the "tube" railways of London are tending towards a universal class throughout Great Britain.

I went to Edinburgh under a three weeks' contract with Sir Henry E. Moss, for his Twentieth Annual Waverley Market Carnival,[1] which opened Boxing Day, December 26, and closed Saturday, January 14. The market is located at the East end of Princes Street, near the post office, in the central part of the city. It occupies a floor space of about 200 feet by 600 feet, with an ornamental terraced roof which is on a level with Princes Street, and laid out in beautiful shrubs and flowers. This annual carnival has been for some time recognized as a national Scottish institution. The main entrance is down the Waverley steps, between the market and the North British Hotel, leading to the Waverley Station, which is the largest in the world. The general admission to the carnival is six pence (12 cents), with six pence extra for a seat, and three pence extra for each side show, of which there were fifteen, ranged on the North side of the hall. On the South side was a huge stage for vaudeville and circus acts, with seats for about 2,000 persons. Amer's Military Band of forty musicians furnished excellent music.

1. Griffin is referring to the Twentieth Annual Waverley Market Carnival (1903–1904), the program for which is in the Theatre Programmes Collection of the National Library of Scotland (MUS 250).

There were gorgeous roundabouts, shooting saloons, photographic galleries, ball games, and stalls of every conceivable kind that go to make a carnival interesting. The doors were open from eleven a.m. until eleven p.m.; the stage performance running from two to five and seven to ten-thirty p.m., with frequent intermissions for the benefit of the side shows.

Sir H. E. Moss, the manager of the carnival, is the B. F. Keith[2] of Great Britain. He is the managing director of the Moss Empires, Ltd., controlling, in addition to the carnival, twenty-seven high class music halls, scattered throughout the kingdom, of which the famous London Hippodrome is the head. His father, James Moss, belonged to an old Lancashire family, and young Moss was, practically speaking, brought up in the business, belonging to that class which we in America would call cross-road showmen. When his father toured with a concert party, young Moss was the accompanist, and sang a humorous song at the piano. Subsequently the elder Mr. Moss became the proprietor of the Horne Music Hall, at Greenock, where he installed his son as manager. At the age of twenty-three he acquired his first music hall, the Gaiety, in Edinburgh. This house had never enjoyed a very savory reputation, and Mr. Moss decided on a revolution. He made one plucky attempt after another to attract respectable people with a purified entertainment, but without success. The climax of

---

2. Benjamin Franklin Keith was a key figure in the development of the American circus industry who later moved into vaudeville as a theater owner before becoming one of the pioneers of the cinema.

his misfortunes came when he organized a great New Year's entertainment in 1878. He spent large sums in advertising, but the result was dire disappointment. Success, however, eventually came, and he has never looked back since.

His son, James, who was married to a daughter of Sir Robert Cranston, the Lord Provost of Edinburgh,[3] died in 1904, at the beginning of a most promising career. This was a terrible blow to Mr. Moss—indeed, he has never seemed quite the same since. He has a younger son, Charles, who has assisted materially in the success of the carnival, and whom we will probably soon see regularly installed in the managerial harness. Hogmanay (New Year's Eve) and New Year's Day are the *premiere* festival days of the year in Scotland. Several years ago the Scotch borrowed the Christmas habit from the English, and even now it seems only a preliminary celebration leading up to the climax of gayety, which is reached on New Year's Day. On the other hand, Englanders are rapidly adopting the Scotch Hogmanay—surely "fair exchange is no robbery." All day Saturday, the last day of the old year, the streets were thronged with people, the weather being *brae* (cold),[4] and I then thought I had never seen so many

3. Sir Robert Cranston served as Lord Provost of Edinburgh, the Scottish equivalent of mayor, from 1903 to 1906.

4. Griffin has almost certainly misunderstood something that he heard here. There is no word "brae" in Scots, Scottish English, or Gaelic with the meaning "cold." A more likely term would be the Scots "braw," generally meaning "good" but sometimes described as deriving from a common root with the English "brave." More likely it is from the Gaelic *breá*, which also means "good." Ironically, poor weather is often referred to in Scotland as being "braw." *Brae* is a Scots term for hill or slope.

drunken persons in my life, but as evening advanced it grew worse, and the debauch continued all night. My lodgings were in Greenside Place, which seemed to be about the centre of the disturbance. It was impossible to sleep on account of the continuous singing and playing of musical instruments, of which the accordion seemed to predominate. "Bill Bailey" and "Blue Bell" are indelibly engraved on my musical memory, as they were the favorite airs. The "pubs" closed at ten o'clock, so they laid in a supply of bottles, and as the hour of midnight drew near they repaired to the Old Tron Kirk, in High Street. As the clock tolled the hour of the new year, they drank the contents and broke the bottle on the walls or on heads that happened to be in the way. The next day, Sunday, was a busy day for the ambulances and hospitals.

As the celebration was continued Sunday and Monday night, sleep was quite out of the question. Monday the crowds were so dense in Princes Street and Waterloo Place that it was nearly impossible to get through, and although the price of admission to the carnival was doubled, the place was packed from ten a.m. until eleven p.m. Tuesday there was another crush, mostly trippers from the surrounding towns. Saturday, Monday and Tuesday, December 31, January 2 and 3, were declared legal holidays, and all business, except that of catering to the holiday crowds, was suspended. But with all the drunkenness, the number of fights and similar infractions of the law were comparatively few. On the whole, I am inclined to the belief that the common people in England have a more wholesome regard for law and order than in the States. I am sorry to say, however, that what amounts almost to a national pastime over there, is wife beating, and the first American that invents a patent[ed] safety lamp that can be thrown across the room without exploding, will, in my humble estimation, reap a rich harvest.

The carnival closed Saturday, January 14. On the fifteenth (being Sunday) I took a much needed rest, but Monday, January 16, I went sight-seeing, and I certainly saw the sights of Edinburgh to my heart's content, so that when night came I felt tired to death, and my head was full of old castles, ruined palaces, monuments and other bric-a-brac too numerous to mention. The first place of interest I visited was Sir Walter Scott's monument, located in the beautiful Princes Street Gardens. It is two hundred feet in height and has a heroic marble statue of the great poet underneath its Gothic arches. It cost about £16,000 ($80,000), and is adorned with statues of prominent characters in Scott's works, and with likenesses of the famous Scottish poet. It was designed by George Meikle Kemp,[5] son of a shepherd on the Pentland Hill, who, when a boy of ten, had his enthusiasm stirred by a visit to Roslin Castle and Chapel, and subsequently devoted many years of his life to the study of Gothic architecture.

5. George Meikle Kemp was a self-taught architect who won a public competition to design the Scott Monument in 1838. Kemp met his death as described by Griffin on the foggy night of March 6, 1844, when he fell into the canal on his way home from the site.

Unfortunately the young architect did not survive to see the work far advanced, being one night accidentally drowned in the Union Canal.

A little further West on Princes Street is the National Gallery. A visit here among such beautiful pictures and artistic statues inspires even *pauvre moi*[6] with a desire to become an artist. The work that impressed me most was an unfinished picture, John Knox dispensing the sacrament at Calderhouse; on the farther side of a long table, which crosses the picture horizontally, stands in the centre the great reformer handing a communion cup to a lady seated at the left Beyond her are others seated at the table, and behind them a bearded man passes with a basket of bread while on the right is a knight with bread in his hand, two men in armor reading from the same book, and others. In the foreground to right and left are more figures, including several children. The head of the reformer and the groups to the right are almost completed, as are two isolated heads on that side and three to the left, but otherwise the figures are only sketched in pencil. There is a pathetic side to this picture which illustrates the uncertainty of human life. The artist, Sir David Wilkie,[7] commenced the picture in 1839. In

---

6. Griffin's attempt at French for "poor me" which, strictly speaking, should be "pauvre de moi."

7. Sir David Wilkie was one of the leading Scots artists of his day. In 1809 Wilkie was elected as associate of the Royal Academy of Edinburgh; in 1823 he became Royal Limner of Scotland as a result of which he was commissioned to paint a portrait of King George IV to commemorate George's visit to Edinburgh the previous year. The painting described by Griffin, which can still be seen in the National Gallery of Scotland, is one of two

1840 he went on a journey to Constantinople, Egypt and the Holy Land, from which he never returned, having died on the homeward voyage. He was buried at sea.

My next stop was at historic, battle scarred Edinburgh Castle, one of the most conspicuous and picturesque citadels in all Europe. Built on a solid granite rock of volcanic origin, it has stood the rack of ages. It covers eleven acres at the bottom, seven acres at the top, and is 443 feet above sea level. The castle rock was probably a favorite post of the ancient Caledonians. The earliest recorded fact, however, is the capture of the fortress in 626, by Edwin, the Saxon king of Northumbria. The walls vary from ten to seventeen feet in thickness, and it strikes one as being well nigh impregnable, but the modern methods of sapping and mining, used so successfully by the Japanese at Port Arthur, would probably reduce it in a short while.

In describing the principal interesting points of the castle, we will commence at the top, which is reached by a steep, winding roadway. Passing through a large court, we enter the old Parliament Hall, now converted into an armory 80 feet by 30 feet and 27 feet in height. Next we inspect Queen Mary's room, where James VI of Scotland and I of England, was born, June 19, 1566. On the Northern parapet we find "Mons Meg,"

---

works in progress featuring the Scots Presbyterian reformer John Knox (unfinished at the time of the artist's death). The other is *John Knox before the Lords of the Congregation*, which is in the Tate Gallery in London.

64   FOUR YEARS IN EUROPE WITH BUFFALO BILL

a relic of the fifteenth century, said to be the largest and oldest piece of ordnance in all Europe. It measures 13 feet in length, 7 feet in circumference, has a calibre of 20 inches, and weighs upwards of five tons. Near the breech is a considerable rent, which occurred in 1662, when firing a salute in honor of the Duke of York, afterwards James VII.[8] Piled up alongside of it are a number of massive stone balls that would barely go into an ordinary sized washtub, said to be some of the identical ones fired from "Meg," and afterwards found on Wardie Moor, three miles distant.

The following is an extract from the chamberlain's roll, in the quaint language of the time: "To certain pioneers for their labour in the mounting of Mons out of her lair to be shot, and for the finding and carrying of her bullets after she was shot, from Wardie Muir, to the Castle, etc., 10 pence" (20 cents); "to the minstrels who played before Mons down the street for 14 pence and for 8 ells of cloth to cover Mons, nine and a quarter pence." A few feet to the rear of Mons we enter St. Margaret's Chapel,[9] the oldest and smallest church in Scotland, sixteen and a half feet by ten and a half feet, and at least eight hundred years old. The crown room, containing the royal regalia; the courtroom and the prison, with its horribly significant chains and

---

8. James VII of Scotland and II of England, who reigned from 1685 to 1688, held the title Duke of York at the time of the visit to which Griffin refers.

9. The chapel is named for Saint Margaret, who became Queen of Scotland upon her marriage to King Malcolm III in 1066. Margaret was canonized by Pope Innocent IV in 1250.

manacles, completed my tour of the castle. The barracks, accommodating about eight hundred soldiers, being modern, I did not visit. From the castle a seven minutes' walk brought me to the National Museum in Chamberlain's Street, where they have everything in natural history from a tiny bug to the skeleton of a whale seventy-eight feet long. My time was only too limited here. So far as my observation goes, however, it is hardly up to our own Metropolitan Museum in New York. Next I walked down to South Bridge Street, passed the old Iron Kirk, across North Bridge, passed the post office, county prison and Calton Hill Cemetery, which contains Lincoln's monument, erected by Scotch-Americans in 1893. A little farther East we inspect the Burns monument, while right opposite, high up on Calton Hill, the Royal Conservatory looks down upon us. Holyrood Palace was the next point of interest; I visited the picture gallery, containing upwards of a hundred portraits of Scottish kings; Lord Darnley's rooms,[10] from which a private stairway leads to Queen Mary's apartments,[11] which have undergone very little change, save by the ravages of time, since

10. Henry Stuart, First Earl of Albany, was the Lord Darnley who became the second husband of his widowed cousin, Mary Queen of Scots, in 1565. Darnley's murder two years later was a key event in Mary's downfall.

11. Mary Stuart, the ill-fated Mary Queen of Scots, reigned from 1542 to 1567, until she was forced to abdicate as a result of an armed uprising in the wake of her nearly immediate marriage to James Hepburn, the fourth Earl of Boswell, after the death of her second husband, Lord Darnley. In 1568 she went into exile in England, where she was effectively held prisoner on the orders of her cousin, Elizabeth I, and ultimately executed in 1587 amid fears of a Catholic conspiracy to overthrow the English monarchy and place Mary on the throne.

they were occupied by that unhappy queen. The bed of Charles I is to be found in the paneled audience chamber, as is also a grate, said to be the first used in Scotland. Still more interesting is Queen Mary's bedroom, with its ancient bed and moldering finery. The Chapel Royal, in ruins, where Queen Mary and Lord Darnley were wedded, and the royal vault, containing the remains of a long line of Scottish kings and queens, restored to their last resting place by the good Queen Victoria. Edinburgh has a population of 300,000, and is a progressive, go-ahead city.

On my return to London I was informed that the Wild West would tour France the coming season, opening at Paris in March. I went at once to the Berlitz School of Languages in Chancery Lane, to see about taking some French lessons. I went into the office and stated my wants in as few words as possible. The old professor looked over his spectacles at me and said: "What part of America do you come from?" I said: "How do you know I come from America?" He replied: "That is sticking out all over you, but you are a puzzle to me at that. Usually I can tell what section of America you come from—East, West, North or South—but in your case I am at sea." Then I told him my business, that I was a traveler, and I was a mystery to him no longer.

CHAPTER VI—1905

*Grand Opening at Paris—A Zigzag Tour of France—
Disease Among the Horses—Tragedie des Chevaux*

I left London for Paris, March 15, to rejoin Buffalo Bill's Wild West for a tour of continental Europe. As our season did not commence until April 2, we had about two weeks for sightseeing.

Our grounds were beautifully laid out in the Champs de Mars (Military Field), midway between the Galerie des Machines and La Tour Eiffel. This historic ground is the site upon which the great Napoleon marshaled his forces, and it is also the scene of all the great Paris expositions.

Our tented city was artistically arranged in national groups, on grassy lawns, with graveled walks, the tents being of the regulation kind used in army field life. The main pavilion was the largest ever used for a similar exhibition, with a seating capacity of 17,000, which was inadequate to accommodate the immense crowds at least twice during every week of our stay in Paris.

Sunday night, June 4, Buffalo Bill's Wild West concluded what may be justly termed the most pleasantly prosperous engagement in the history of the white tents.

17. Two views of The Wild West in Paris, 1905.

Colonel Cody, a Hawkeye by birth, is personally lionized by the Parisians, and his unique exhibition, so full of historical and dramatic interest, made a wonderful impression upon the susceptible French public.

The twenty lessons I took in French, at the Berlitz School of Languages, London, only gave me a faint idea of what the language was like, but as I was required to make my lectures and announcements in French, I had my speeches translated, and was coached in their delivery by Monsieur Corthésy, *éditeur, le Journal de Londres*. Well, I got along pretty fair, considering that I did not know the meaning of half the words I was saying. Anyway it amused them, so I was satisfied. I honestly believe that more people came in the side show in Paris to hear and laugh at my "rotten" French than anything else, and when I found that a certain word or expression excited their risibilities, I never changed it. I can look back now and see where some of my own literal translations were very funny.

Colonel Cody's exhibition is unique in many ways, and might justly be termed a polyglot school, no less than twelve distinct languages being spoken in the camp, viz.: Japanese, Russian, French, Arabic, Greek, Hungarian, German, Italian, Spanish, Holland, Flemish, Chinese, Sioux and English. Being in such close contact every day, we were bound to get some idea of each other's tongue, and all acquire a fair idea of English. Colonel Cody is, therefore, entitled to considerable credit for disseminating English, and thus preserving the *entente cordiale* between nations.

18. Entrance to the Wild West, Champs de Mars, Paris, 1905.

The first place of public interest that we visited in Paris was the Jardin des Plantes (botanical and zoological garden) and le Musée d'Histoire Naturelle. The zoological collection would suffer in comparison with several in America I might mention, but the Natural History Museum is very complete, and is, to my notion, the most artistically arranged of any museum I have visited.

Le Palais du Trocadéro, which was in sight of our grounds and facing the Champs de Mars, is filled with art treasures dating from the early ages up to the present time. L'Hotel des Invalides contains relics of past wars and illustrates the glories of *le militaire de France*.

Adjoining the great War Museum is a magnificent chapel, surmounted by a great gilded dome, under which rests the mortal remains of the great Napoleon, while in a circle around his tomb lie the ashes of his relatives and generals.

From *le grand roue* (the big wheel) in the Avenue de Suffren, which overlooked our camp, you could get an excellent bird's-eye view of Paris. Connected with the big wheel were a music hall, *café* and ballroom. On one of my visits there I enjoyed the rare privilege of seeing a real French duel between two rival editors. Now, do not think that I am a bloodthirsty wretch who delights to revel in gory bull fights, etc. On the contrary, this was funny. The weapons were swords, they were desperately in earnest, each one must have expected to be killed, as each one had brought a physician. After a few feints one was scratched on the back of the hand, drawing a few drops of blood, and thus outraged honor was satisfied. Of course we all went up in la Tour Eiffel, which was virtually in our front yard. It is curious what different sensations are experienced by those who make the ascension. Some become exhilarated, while it makes others actually ill. Some seem possessed of a hypnotic desire to jump off into space, while others are indifferent to any but ordinary feelings. The tower is 991 feet high, and the base covers seven acres. The more you see and study it the more beautiful it becomes. It is so gracefully symmetrical in its proportions that it seems to be architecturally perfect.

There are two classes of people in Paris; one class is there for the sole purpose of making money, and the other class to spend it. They are both working overtime, and as a result you pay top prices for everything. They do not seem to have regular prices for their goods, but go on the principle that "a sucker is good for all that he will stand for."

The French people are overflowing with experimental energy, and I have no doubt but that some day they will solve the aeronautic problem. One day I witnessed a balloon race in which there were eight contestants; in fact, there was scarcely a day passed but that there was one or more balloons hovering over the Wild West Show grounds.

What seems to be the principal fault of the French people—or rather the Parisian—is their extreme excitability and social immorality. Paris, being a cosmopolitan city, a city almost entirely given up to pleasure, is corrupted by foreign contact, inasmuch as they cater to the vicious tastes of the idle rich of all nations, therefore it is a wonder that it is not worse than it is.

One day a few hundred students in the Boulevard St. Germain, who had a grievance against one of the maîtres,[1] were making a public demonstration, and were dispersed by the *gendarmes*,[2] who handled some of the rioters rather severely. The next day they made their appearance again, in increased numbers, and marched to the office of the prefect of police, who received them politely—a Frenchman is polite, above all things—made a diplomatic speech denouncing the

1. French for "masters."
2. French for "police."

former action of his subordinates, and in a few minutes they were marching down street, cheering for the police just like a lot of capricious children.

The boulevards are broad, well paved and kept remarkably clean. The pavements in front of the *cafés* are almost blocked with chairs and little round tables, at which men and women sit day and night, sipping their wine or *pernod* (absinthe). There are a lot of low grade men there who are supported by hardworking women. One day a woman was pointed out to me in the street pulling a baker's wagon almost as large as a house, while her husband was seated at one of these tables, drinking wine with a gaily dressed woman of the street.

Most of these tradesmen's carts have one or more dogs harnessed to the axle, who really and quite cheerfully, it seems, do all the work, while the man or woman does the guiding.

They drink wine at their meals instead of tea or coffee, and although immense quantities of it are consumed, they seldom drink between meals, and there is much less drunkenness there than in Great Britain or America.

The French women do not possess the natural beauty and splendid physique of the English and American women, but they have a knack of arranging costumes and toilets to make themselves very attractive for the *minimum d'argent*,[3] and some very beautiful and unique toilets are to be seen there.

3. French for the "minimum money."

Although Paris was both beautiful and interesting, when we gave our farewell performance on the Champs de Mars, night of June 4, and went to bed in our own sleeping cars, to wake up many miles away, we were indeed a happy lot. Why? Because nine weeks is too prolonged a stay in any one place for those accustomed to one-day stand circus life in America.

Our first stop out of Paris was at Chartres, a *ville* of 5,000 inhabitants, fifty-five miles Southwest of Paris. The change was indeed refreshing. Instead of the Eiffel Tower, the big wheel, the huge Galerie des Machines and the red sand of the Champs de Mars, we were greeted with growing grass, green trees and running streams. There we had an opportunity of seeing the difference between the cosmopolitan Parisian and the true French provincial, the latter reminding us very much of the happy country circus crowds at home. We stopped one day each at Alençon, Fleurs, St. Lô and Cherbourg, in Normandy. Our stay in the latter city should have been longer, as it is one of the principal seaports of France, and in spite of the cold, drizzling rain which prevailed all day, thousands of people were turned away at both performances.

Rouen, where we exhibited June 15 and 16, on the Champs de Mars, is an interesting old world city of 116,000 inhabitants. I took some snapshots here of the great cathedral, 1,100 years old, and the swinging bridge across the River Seine, which is a great architectural curiosity. Two iron pillars about one hundred feet high support a span across the river; on this is a trolley carrying a sort of car from side to side within a few feet of the water. It is the conception of an English mind, and is, in my mind, only a freak of engineering skill.

The giant clock which is carved in stone over an arch in the Rue du Gros Horloge is another mechanical oddity built in the eighteenth century.

Our next stop was at Le Havre for two days. This is an important seaport on the English Channel. We were billed there for four performances, but on account of a long haul and a soft lot the afternoon performance on the first day and the evening performance of the last day were abandoned.

At Arras, June 23, we saw a mammoth Wild West poster in the Cathedral entrance—rather a unique sight to us Westerners.

We stopped one day each at Douai, Calais and Boulogne, all seaports on the English Channel.[4] At Boulogne the fisher folk in their quaint costumes reminded us of Bonnie Scotland. We occupied the entire market place for our tents, which enclosed a large cathedral. We had barely got our canvas enclosure erected when a funeral applied for admission, but they finally decided to drive on to another church.

June 28 found us at Armentières, in the extreme North of France, on the Belgian border. Tobacco in France is a government monopoly, the prices are high for an inferior quality, and many of the boys took

---

4. Griffin is mistaken here. Calais and Boulogne are seaports but Douai is well inland.

advantage of the cheap and superior quality over the border. The solitary oarsman operating the only ferry across the narrow river did a thriving business all day. He capsized one boatload, to the great amusement of those on shore.

July 1 to 4, inclusive, we spent at Lille, a prosperous silk manufacturing city of 210,000 inhabitants. July 4 we celebrated our national holiday. The entire encampment was gorgeously decorated in tri-colored bunting, a grand banquet was served to the members of the company, the bands played patriotic airs, and Colonel Cody (Buffalo Bill) made one of his characteristic speeches, in which he eulogized the French nation for the important part they had played in American history. James A. Bailey, "the little Napoleon of the show business," and his able lieutenant, George O. Starr,[5] were visitors. This was the last time we saw Mr. Bailey alive.

July 11 to 13 we exhibited at Reims, in the centre of the great champagne district. The city is undermined with huge wine vaults, excavated out of the solid chalk. Many of those in the company who had never tasted champagne before took advantage of its cheapness, and succeeded in getting on a seven dollar "jag" for thirty cents.

At Charleville, July 14, we had an opportunity of seeing how the French people celebrate their national independence day. This is equivalent to our Fourth

---

5. George Starr was Bailey's business partner from 1899 to the time of his death.

of July, and commemorates the fall of the Bastille. Charleville-Mezzier was sacked and burned by the Germans in 1871, and the village still shows signs of that memorable struggle.

The next day, July 15, we exhibited on the Champs de Mars, Sedan, where Napoleon III met defeat in 1870.[6]

During the month of July we traveled along the Belgian, German and Swiss frontiers, and as these towns were all well fortified, our audiences, in many instances, were more than half military, who were accorded a reduced rate, that being a national custom. They are a well behaved lot of fellows, being composed of all classes, the conscript system being in vogue—doctors, lawyers, tradesmen, mechanics, *et al.*, all being liable to three years' service, for which they receive pay at the rate of *un sou* (1 cent) per day. The rations are barely enough to sustain life, and if the poor soldier has no money or friends, he has a sorry time of it indeed.

At Lunéville, July 21, our camp was pitched in a basin, surrounded by hills or mountains, which formed a great natural amphitheatre, from which those who had neither the price nor the inclination to pay, could, and did, view the performance gratis. "Grand stand

---

6. The army of Napoleon III, Charles-Louis-Napoléon Bonaparte, the nephew of the Emperor Napoleon Bonaparte (who was both the first president of the French Republic and the last monarch of France), was defeated at Sedan on September 1, 1870, by the Prussian Army in one of the decisive actions of the Franco-Prussian War. Napoleon III was taken prisoner by the Prussians the following day.

19. The Wild West in Rouen, France, 1905.

hill" was lined with French soldiers, whose red caps and trousers, blue coats and white over-gaiters, with the green grass for a background, formed a unique picture, full of color.

August 4 we began a ten days' stay at Lyons, the third city of France, with a population of nearly 500,000. Lyons is celebrated for the manufacture of silks.

Sunday, August 20, was a gala day at Vichy, the Saratoga of France, where the Shah of Persia[7] and *suite*, numbering about fifty persons, honored us with a visit.

7. Mozaffar al-Din Shah Qajar was the fifth Shah of Persia from the Qajar Dynasty between 1853 and 1907. Cody's own account of his encounter with the Shah was published in the *Philadelphia Press Sunday Magazine*, May 12, 1907, p. 8.

There were fully 17,000 people present, and when Colonel Cody shook hands with His Highness, the applause was tremendous. The Comtesse de Paris[8] and party occupied a private box on the same occasion. If France were still a monarchy she would probably be the reigning queen, as she is next in line of succession.

En route from Riom to Montluçon, August 22, one of our huge stock cars was derailed by a misplaced switch. The railway force labored for about two hours to replace it, without success. Finally our crew of "razor-backs" came to the rescue, and had the car on the track in fifteen minutes.

As a whole, the railway service in France is good, but the wages are very low. My opinion is that those who are most in favor of government ownership of railroads in America would be the first to complain were the present order of things reversed.

We had some terrific storms during the season, but the most severe of all struck us at Orléans, August 25. It completely demolished the big tent, and scores of people were more or less injured, but none fatally.

On the morning of August 24, by special invitation, we visited the Exposition, which had been running

8. Marie-Isabelle d'Orléans, Comtesse de Paris, was the widow of Louis-Philippe d'Orléans, a claimant to the French throne under the putative title of Philippe VII of the House of Orléans. Although an extremely distinguished royal personage of the sort whose patronage was courted by Cody—she was the granddaughter of two kings, Louis-Philippe I of France and Ferdinand VII of Spain—Griffin is wrong to assert that Marie-Isabelle would have been the reigning queen of France if the country were still a monarchy. Her son, Philippe d'Orléans, was the claimant to the French throne from that particular royal house at the time, under the putative title of Philippe VIII, and the Comtesse would therefore have been Queen Mother.

here since May. Among its most interesting features were le Village Noir (the Black City), composed of ninety Senegals, from the French colonies in Africa.

On every hand we are reminded by beautiful paintings, sculpture and marked historical spots that this was the birthplace of Joan of Arc.

Wednesday, August 30, we viewed the partial eclipse of the sun at Thouars. This unusual spectacle was followed by a terrific electric storm, lasting about twenty minutes. Lightning struck one of the Wild West horse tents and instantly killed four horses, among them the two valuable white Arabians which Colonel Cody drove to his private carriage. Several of the attaches of the stable department suffered from shock, but none were seriously injured.

At Quimper, September 11, we encountered an English colony with a lot of excursionists from the Isle of Jersey. It seemed strange indeed to have people ask us questions in English, and after wrestling with a foreign language so long, we were almost at a loss to form sentences in our native tongue.

Morning of September 12 we were treated to a beautiful view of the harbor of Brest, with the formidable French fleet at anchor. Here is where the English and French navies had their fraternal maneuvers to seal the *entente cordiale*,[9] which has been of immense

---

9. The French term "entente cordiale," meaning "cordial understanding," was used extensively in the publicity for the Wild West's 1905 tour of France and was used to emphasize the historically friendly relations between the United States and France, which dated back to the time of the American Revolution.

value to France in a commercial way. The English forgot their old resolve to stay at home and spend their holiday money and flocked to the French resorts by the thousands. My friend, Sydney Wire, writing me from Paris at the time, said: "Never in its history has the French capital been so engulfed with English-speaking people."

At Saint-Malo, September 14, we had another big crowd of English visitors from the Channel Islands.

September 15 found us at Rennes, where the final chapter in the Dreyfus[10] case was enacted. The Palais de Justice, where he received his final pardon, was close to the show ground and was visited by many of the show people.

Bordeaux, with a population of 256,638, was the next large city we visited, making a ten days' stay there on the beautiful Place des Quinconces, situated in the heart of the city. Well, it would be equivalent to Union Square in New York City, surrounded by beautiful statues, heroic monuments, sparkling fountains and everything that goes to make a public park attractive. At the back or rear entrance was the river and wharf, with its varied shipping, the huge barges

---

10. The Dreyfus case was a hugely controversial political scandal in turn-of-the-century France. Jewish captain Alfred Dreyfus was wrongly convicted of being a German spy and evidence of his innocence was suppressed by high-ranking military officials in what was later to be seen as an anti-Semitic coverup. After the intervention of Emile Zola in an open letter to the newspaper *L'Aurore* (January 23, 1898), Dreyfus was granted a retrial and again convicted, although this time sentenced to ten years hard labor rather than life imprisonment. He received the final pardon to which Griffin refers in April 1906. For detailed accounts of the case see in particular Bredin (1986) and Whyte (2008).

20. Group of Senegalese, and a mother and son, Orléans, 1905.

of wine casks being mainly in evidence. Broad stone steps lead up to the grounds between two ancient stone towers representing commerce. Standing almost in the side show door was a magnificent gray stone soldiers' monument, about two hundred feet high, one of the finest in all France, "A la mémoire des Girondins."[11] At the base of this monument, on either side, are beautiful bronze marine groups of statuary representing peace and progress. One block to the East of us was the beautiful Theatre Municipal, and to the South, a short block, was a fine monument in memory of and surmounted by a heroic statue of "Gambetta,[12] *Père du Pays*" (Father of the Country). October 1, our last day at Bordeaux, was celebrated by many of us going aux Arènes Espagnoles[13] to see a Spanish bull fight. All were unanimous in declaring it to be the most beastly and blood-thirsty exhibition they had ever seen. There is a law against bull fighting in France, and as the bull ring is located on city property the aldermen are solemnly brought to justice every Monday morning (bull fights always take place on Sunday) and fined 16 francs ($3.20).

11. The Girondins were a republican faction at the time of the French Revolution, a group that got its name from the fact that a significant proportion of its representatives in the Legislative Assembly and the National Convention came from the region of the Gironde.

12. Léon Gambetta, the son of an Italian immigrant grocer, was a French radical politician who rose from his humble origins through the ranks of the law to ultimately serve as prime minister from 1881 to 1882. The statue referred to by Griffin was unveiled by the president of France in April 1905 and can still be seen in the Place Gambetta in Bordeaux.

13. French for "to the Spanish arenas."

Four days after our departure from Bordeaux, the annual *fête* or fair, one of the largest in France, held in honor of the grape harvest, was given on the grounds we occupied. La Société des Forains (the society of open air showmen) made a desperate fight to keep the Wild West out of Bordeaux, but without avail. They boycotted and scandalized us in every conceivable way, but despite that fact, and that it rained torrents eight of the ten days we were there, we did a good paying business.

October 3 we showed at Bayonne, only two miles from Biarritz, the famous coast resort, and twenty-five miles from the Spanish main. The little blue, toboggan-like caps told us plainly that our audience was composed mainly of Spaniards. It is a strongly fortified place, in remembrance of the many bloody wars between France and Spain in the misty past. There are miles and miles of stone masonry, and the city is completely surrounded by a moat which could be flooded with water in case of attack.

At Pau, October 4, we got our first glimpse of the Lower Pyrenees. It is a great Winter resort of English and American tourists. *En route* from Pau to Tarbes, thirty-seven miles, we passed Lourdes, famous for cures of the faithful. There we had a fine view of the Upper Pyrenees, including le pic du Midi, or South peak (10,000 feet), which was covered with this year's snow, and as there was a strong wind from that direction, we nearly perished with the cold. Although the show ground was five kilometres from the city, and a drizzling rain prevailed, we had two immense audiences.

October 6, at Mont de Marsan, our tents were pitched on the racetrack, surrounded by a turpentine grove, five miles from town, and only cabs and carry-alls to convey the crowds to and from the show—well, many of us had to ride "Shank's ponies."

October 9 we stopped at Bergerac, where Monsieur Rostand dug up his quaint character of Cyrano.[14] The ancient chateau of the great fighter is one of the interesting relics that link the past with the present.

At Béziers, October 21, 22, we occupied the military field, adjoining which was the bull ring, one of the largest and finest we had seen, built of red brick in circular form, with a seating capacity for 12,000 people. It is a noticeable fact that where we find these bull rings, the people seem to partake of the savagery they suggest. Only a short time before we were there the audience tore up and set fire to the benches because the management refused to kill another bull, after already killing six, the advertised number. After a bull fight the carcasses are cut up and sold to the people for food. Is it any wonder that such people are savage?

October 23 we were on the shores of the Mediterranean, at Sète. The Hooligan element was very much in evidence there, reminding one of the early days in

14. Hector Savinien de Cyrano de Bergerac, a seventeenth-century French dramatist and noted duelist, is now better known on account of the literary character loosely based on his life in the 1897 play, *Cyrano de Bergerac*, by Edmond Eugène Alexis Rostand.

21. The Tragedie des Chevaux (*top*), and a sad farewell.

America, when the "bad" element of a section regarded the advent of a circus as an intrusion or menace, and would attack the show people for no other reason than that they were strangers. One of their favorite pastimes on this occasion was throwing stones at the drivers, out of the darkness. Finally it became necessary to charge them on horseback, and they proved to be a bunch of arrant cowards, as is usual in such cases. At least a dozen of them will never forget the Wild West. Sète is a city of 35,000 population and a fortress of the *première classe*.

October 27 found us at the ancient city of Nîmes, rich in Roman antiquities. When Colonel Cody and the Wild West were here in 1889[15] they exhibited a month in the old stone arena, which is almost as ancient as the Colosseum at Rome, and built on the same lines. Several of "our boys" had their pictures taken there. Considering its great age, it is still in a good state of preservation, being in use now as a bull ring.

October 30 we exhibited at Arles, another old Roman town much frequented by tourists. The arena here, which is still used as a bull ring, was built in the year 400 B.C.

November 1 we arrived at Marseille, our goal. We closed the season of 1905 November 12, at which time an audience of 15,000 people assembled to see the farewell performance. The season was a most arduous

---

15. Griffin is mistaken here. The Wild West did not appear in Nîmes in 1889. The show's 1889 dates in France were: Paris (May 18 to November 14); Lyon (November 17 to November 28); and Marseille (December 1 to December 16).

one, seven and one-half months' continuous showing without a Sunday's rest to break the monotony. Besides the ordinary trials of a showman's life we had opposition with another big American institution, McCaddon's International Shows,[16] featuring a Wild West, and, worst of all,

La Tragedie des Chevaux.

Shortly after leaving Paris glanders broke out among the broncos, and government veterinaries were placed with us to combat the dread disease. Forty-two horses were taken out and shot in one day.

When we closed the season at Marseille we only had about one hundred broncos left to give the performance, two hundred having been killed during the season.

Our magnificent draught stock, which was under the care of Jake Posey, of Cincinnati, never came in contact with the broncos, so they did not become contaminated. When the show was finally put away in Winter quarters, Mr. Bailey and Colonel Cody, equal owners of the Wild West, held a consultation, and it

16. Polacsek (1982) gives an account of McCaddon's ill-fated 1905 International Show. Joseph Terry McCaddon was a crucial figure in turn of the century American circus. He began his career as manager of the Adam Forepaugh Circus and was later the business manager of his brother-in-law's troupe, the James A. Bailey's Barnum and Bailey Circus (McCaddon's sister, Ruth McCaddon, was Bailey's wife). He represented Bailey in many business matters, including correspondence with Cody regarding the acquisition of the Wild West Show. Many of McCaddon's papers are held as the McCaddon Collection at Princeton University Library. Scrapbook 14 and Boxes 41 and 42 are of particular relevance for his dealings with Cody.

was decided to kill the remaining hundred broncos and burn all the trappings, that being the only way of stamping out the plague, and importing new broncos and trappings from America for the next season. After the first batch of forty-two horses were taken out and shot I took a long article, written for the American press, to Fred. B. Hutchinson,[17] the manager, asking for his approval. He read it carefully, knit his brows a little and handed it back to me, saying, "Charlie, the least said about this the better;" hence the story has never been publicly told until now.

17. Fred Bailey Hutchinson, a long-standing director of the Barnum and Bailey Circus, acted as a manager with the Wild West for several seasons and went on to work with the Sells-Floto Show.

CHAPTER VII—WINTER 1905–1906
Marseille, the Gateway to the Orient—Wintering Under Canvas—More Observations of French Manners and Customs

From November, 1905, until March, 1906, we wintered under canvas at Marseille, the semi-tropical climate of that latitude rendering such a heretofore unheard of proposition possible. When Manager Fred Hutchinson first spoke of doing this, the old boys shook their heads, but Colonel Cody, having full confidence in his young manager, after pulling us safely through one of the most strenuous seasons ever experienced by any show, thought "Freddy" knew best—and "Freddy" did know best. "All's well that ends well," and Mr. Hutchinson received great credit from everyone for his forethought in saving the firm a lot of trouble and expense.

Marseille is the most important seaport of France, having one of the finest harbors in the world and a population of 500,000. You get an excellent *vue d'oiseau*[1] of the city from L'Eglise Notre-Dame de la Garde,[2] which is situated on a rocky promontory 500 feet above the sea. The chapel is surmounted by a steeple 150 feet

---

1. French for "bird's-eye view."
2. The Neo-Byzantine Basilica de Notre-Dame de la Garde stands on a limestone promontory to the south of Marseille harbor and does afford excellent panoramic views over the city referred to by Griffin.

22. *A Visit to the Chateau d'If—Monte Cristo Island.* 1—*The starting point, Old Harbor, Marseilles.* 2—*A view of the island from a distance.* 3—*Looking through prison bars toward Marseilles.*

high, supporting a huge bronze statue of the Madonna, which is out of all proportion to the size of the main structure, which gives it a peculiarly odd appearance. There is also in the same enclosure a battery of artillery, soldiers' barracks, a government signal station and a café restaurant. On the occasion of my visit services were being held, and the music from the splendid choir and big organ was particularly impressive.

On the North from Notre Dame, extending in a semi-circle around the city, are the Maritime Alps, while on the South you have a fine view of the Mediterranean and the extensive harbor, filled with ships of every nationality, all of which is set off by several rocky islets, on the smallest of which is that famous fortress, the Chateau d'If,[3] from whence the great

---

[3]. The island of If is the smallest island in the Frioul Archipelago in the bay of Marseille and the sixteenth-century chateau there, which was later used as a prison, is as described by Griffin. It is still visited by tourists, mainly due to its association with the 1844 adventure novel by Alexandre Dumas, *The Count of Monte Cristo.*

Dumas took his inimitable character of Monte Cristo. For one franc you can visit this island in a comfortable steam launch, see the ancient prisons and the dungeon where Edmund Dantès was imprisoned, and at the same time get a sensation of *mal de mer*[4] if you are not a good sailor.

Leaving Notre Dame by winding stone steps, we go down through Pharo Park, where the Pasteur Institute, Medical College and Morgue are situated, also getting a closer view of the dock and the Transborder Bridge. Then we come to the Cannebière, the literal meaning of which is a tub of beer. This is the main "stem" of the city from which all the principal *rues* radiate, and is a busy place at all times. This is the particular pride of the Marseillian, who says: "Paris would be a very nice place if they only had la Cannebière."

I never saw so much bad coin in my life as in France, and particularly Marseille. It is not considered bad form to pass out a counterfeit piece if you have been unwise enough to accept one. The government does not seem to make any effort to keep bad money out of circulation. If you tender a bad coin at the post office or bank, they merely hand it back, saying *"Pas bon."*[5]

Everyone in France has a little money—even the beggars have money in bank usually, because they make a business of it.

A golden rule in French pronunciation is, pronounce a word any old way except the way that it is spelled.

4. French for "seasickness."
5. French for "not good."

23. *In Winter Quarters, Marseille, France, 1905–6.*

The respect shown the dead by the French people is commendable. No matter what a person has been or done in life, all is forgotten in death. When a funeral cortege passes through the street everybody stops and uncovers his head. The cemeteries are carefully attended and are a thing of beauty. The *première classe* (there are eight classes of funerals) are placed in vaults underground, surmounted by a small chapel containing a shrine, with photographs of the dead all beautifully decorated with flowers, real or artificial. Bread is their staff of life, and wine is cheap. Their bread is the best in the world and costs about 20 *centimes*, or 4 cents per *demi kilo* (one pound), for the best quality. When the Germans invaded France in 1870–71 the soldiers wrote back home: "This is a great country; the people

24. *Working under the Southern Sun, December, 1905.*

eat cake all the time," their bread being so different from the black or brown bread which they were accustomed to at home. A cheaper quality of bread is baked in huge loaves as large as a washtub. One cent's worth of this bread and a half *litre* of cheap, sour wine, which costs one cent, will make a substantial meal for a working man. Almost every other food is dearer there than here or England. Good bacon costs forty cents a pound; sugar, seven cents; milk, eight cents; ham, $1.00.

There is not the same standard of home life in France as we have in America or England, as is attested by the *cafés* and restaurants everywhere. They will eat bread and drink a little wine three or four times a day at home and all go out to a restaurant for dinner. You can get a fair six course dinner there, including tea, coffee, milk or wine, for thirty cents, or by purchasing ten tickets you may have it for twenty-five cents a meal. Day board, by the month, $12.00. I never had as good a French dinner in all France as I used to get for fifty cents at a French restaurant in Twenty-eighth Street, New York, kept by one "Spanish John," who, by the way, happened to be an Italian.

An ordinary shave costs you three cents, and haircutting is four cents. After *le barbier* has lathered and shaved you, it is your turn to go to the wash bowl, wash the lather off, return to the chair and he finishes the job.

The South of France is much like parts of our own South, primitive and behind the times. Their *patois* is a mixture of French, Spanish and Italian. They are very excitable and passionate. They work milk cows like oxen, and their horses, which are very small, are yoked together.

25. Winter quarters at Marseille, France (1905)

26. The staff in winter quarters, and Cody's two favorite horses.

27. The office at winter quarters in Marseille, and
F. B. Hutchinson having a go at lawn tennis.

CHAPTER VIII—1906

Opening of the Season at Marseille—Tour of Italy, Austria-Hungary, Germany and Belgium

Buffalo Bill's Wild West inaugurated their twenty-fourth annual tour at Marseille, France, March 4, 1906, on the same grounds where we closed our 1905 tour, and where the show was wintered.

The first week out, beginning at Marseille, March 4, and ending at Nice, March 10, was the biggest opening week, financially, in the history of the show. While we were at Nice everybody had the Monte Carlo fever, and the boys tell some amusing tales of "how they did not break the bank."

March 13 was cut out to make the run from Nice to Genoa, Italy, which, to my notion, was the most beautiful route ever traversed by a show train. On one side of us was the blue Mediterranean, and on the other were high mountains, full of snow. The almond trees were full of fragrant blossoms.

During the run Colonel Cody sat on the observation platform of his private car and received a perfect ovation from immense throngs of people at every *stazione*. The formalities of the customs were all arranged in advance by General Agent Clarence L. Dean,[1] so

1. Clarence L. Dean had been advance agent for Barnum and Bailey's earlier tour of Europe and joined the Wild West in the same capacity for the 1902–1906 tours.

28. *Street Scene, Genoa, Italy, March, 1906.*

we experienced no delay on that score. We were in four sections, the last one arriving at Genoa at two p.m., or, according to the Italian system of reckoning time, fourteen o'clock (twenty-four o'clock being midnight).

Our first performance was given at Genoa, afternoon of 14, and thousands of people were turned away, and the side show—well, many circuses would be "tickled to death" to do the business that our side show did. Morning of 15 two new 60 feet middle pieces were put up, thus adding considerably to our seating capacity, and yet thousands were unable to gain admission. It is my humble opinion that we should have remained at Genoa at least a week.

Genoa, the birthplace of Columbus, is one of the most beautiful cities I have visited anywhere. The English fleet was at anchor while we were there. Lord Charles Beresford[2] and about 2,000 jackies[3] attended the performance, night of 16.

La Spezia, March 17, was one day only, and then we filled our immense amphitheatre for two performances with country people whose enthusiastic applause seemed to have no bound.

Livorno, 18, 19, 20, during the celebration of the three hundredth anniversary of the city government, was to big business at every performance. Evening of 19 a strong wind came up at about six o'clock, and the night show had to be abandoned, which gave many of us an opportunity of witnessing a magnificent display of fireworks by the city.

March 21 we made the run from Livorno to Rome, a distance of 334 kilometres (205¾ miles). The last section left Livorno at five o'clock a.m., crossed the Tiber at seventeen-thirty, and entered the capital city at eighteen o'clock, according to Roman time.

Never in the twenty-four years' history of the Wild West was there such a crowd of people to welcome its arrival. The streets were blocked and traffic suspended in the vicinity of the station. The police reserves were

---

2. Charles William de la Poer Beresford, First Baron Beresford, known at the time as Lord Charles Beresford, was admiral in command of the British Mediterranean Fleet in 1906. Prominent both as a naval commander and politician, his autobiography is available online at www.archive.org.
3. The term "jackies" was used colloquially to mean British sailors.

called out, and they finally cleared the way for us to the Piazza d'Armi, where we were to exhibit.

Sunday, March 25, the Wild West was honored by a visit from the King and Queen of Italy,[4] Count of Turin, Count and Countess Guicciardini, and the members of the court. After witnessing the spectacle throughout, King Victor Emanuel commanded a private performance for the following day. Punctually at ten o'clock their majesties arrived, accompanied by their children and suite. The royal audience heartily applauded the performance, and Colonel Cody received the personal congratulations of the king, also a gold cigarette case, with the royal monogram and crest, studded with diamonds, and a beautifully worded letter, thanking him for both performances.

Morning of March 27 Press Agent Frank A. Small, who, by the way, is the biggest Small you ever saw, standing nearly seven feet tall, received the following characteristic telegram from George Ade[5]: "Six hungry Yanks will be on the lot at noon; notify the cook tent."

The party included George Ade, the Sultan of Sulu; Booth Tarkington, the Gentleman from Indiana; Mr.

4. The Italian monarchs who visited the Wild West were Victor Emmanuel III, King of Italy from 1900 to 1947 and his wife, Queen Helen of Montenegro. The Count of Turin was the king's nephew, Victor Emmanuel of Savoia-Aosta and Count Francesco Guicciardini was his Minister of Foreign Affairs at that time and his wife was Maria Luisa, Countess Bombicci Pontelli. Cody's own more extensive account of the Italian Royal visit was published in the *Philadelphia Press Sunday Magazine*, May 12, 1907, p. 8.

5. George Ade was a leading newspaper columnist who went on to distinction as an essayist, humorist, and playwright. In *The Sultan of Sulu*, first produced in 1902, he satirized the figure of an American abroad.

Thompson, Mr. Sweet, *et al*.[6] They were not only after something to eat, but were in search of material for their literary work, and I guess they got it. Anyway, they had the run of the show and seemed to be having a jolly good time. Mr. Ade presented the snake charmer in the Side Show with a box of bon bons. "The bravest little lady in the land" untied the string, and—had a snake fit. Instead of bon bons the package contained a large spiral spring snake, about nine feet long. Ade was very industrious all day trying to spend an American paper dollar among the privilege people. Frank S. Griffin[7] was the first one to turn it down; Frank remembered him from the Ringling Show when Ade was a regular trouper. But I think the sight of that dollar bill made Frank homesick, as he left a "good thing" and returned to the States a few days later. Hall Caine[8] was also among our distinguished guests at Rome.

Rome has a population of 500,000, and is the most interesting city, historically, in all Europe. Whole libraries of books are published descriptive of its wonders, and as every encyclopedia tells of its past glories, I will not attempt to describe with my feeble powers

6. Newton Booth Tarkington was a prominent writer who won the Pulitzer Prize for his novels *The Magnificent Ambersons* and *Alice Adams*.
    It has not been possible to identify the other two Americans named by Griffin. In Cody's own account of the incident (from the *Philadelphia Press Sunday Magazine*, May 12, 1907, p. 7), other members of the party were simply "American tourists."
7. The author's brother.
8. Sir Thomas Henry Hall Caine was one of the leading English novelists of the late nineteenth and early twentieth centuries.

29. Opening day in Rome, March 22, 1906.

of description its manifold wonders. Suffice to say we visited the Colosseum, Pantheon, Quirinal, etc., and were not disappointed.

All through April the weather was abnormally warm, even for Italy. Many attributed this to the eruptions of Vesuvius.[9] We were never nearer than two hundred miles to the active volcano, but we had several scares and everything was made ship-shape as for a big storm, which turned out to be clouds of red dust, while the supposed lightning was also from old Vesuvius.

All kinds of bad things were predicted for us in Italy, and many of us had it down as a land of anarchists, with bombs and stilettos, but we found the

9. The volcano Vesuvius, which overlooks the Bay of Naples in southern Italy.

people the most peaceable and more subject to police control than any country we visited outside of England. The police, too, are a fine looking and efficient body of men.

We bade farewell to sunny Italy with many regrets, and crossed over into Austria, at Trieste,[10] May 12, where we remained for four days to capacity business. Trieste has a population of about 40,000, and is a seaport of considerable importance. It formerly belonged to Italy, and two-thirds of the population are Italians. Although German is the official language, the people will not stand for the Austrian flag or speak the German language.

May 17 and 18 found us in the quaint city of Agram,[11] capital of Croatia. Although they have their own language, parliament, government officials and revenues, they are under the protection of Austria. In 1886 Agram was totally destroyed by an earthquake, but now it is a very beautiful and substantial city of 20,000 happy and contented inhabitants. The State Theatre, which is maintained by the government for the perpetuation of the Croatian language, is a particularly attractive structure, almost on a par with the Grand Opera House at Paris.

From Agram we went up through the picturesque Austrian Tyrol to Vienna (1,800,000 population) on

10. Trieste is now part of Italy and has been since the 1919 Treaty of Versailles. A detailed account (in Italian) of the Wild West's time in the city can be found in Stern (1994).
11. Currently Zagreb, Croatia. The appendix to this volume gives the current names and national affiliations of all of the venues in the former Austro-Hungarian Empire visited by the Wild West in 1906.

FOUR YEARS IN EUROPE WITH BUFFALO BILL

30. A bunch of the Wild West taken in the old Colosseum, Rome.

the Danube. We played a most successful three weeks' engagement on the Prater,[12] at the very doors of the Great Rotunda, a relic of the Exposition of 1878. There was scarcely one out of the forty days at Vienna that we did not entertain royalty. Doubtless we could have remained there all Summer and made money.

When Colonel Cody visited Vienna in 1900, the Grand Duke Frederick[13] was skeptical about the genuineness of the wild horses in the bucking act, and being a gruff old fellow, was not backward at all about saying so, whereupon the Colonel invited him to a

12. The Wiener Prater is a large public park in Vienna and the site of the famous Wurstelprater amusement park.
13. Archduke Frederick Maria Albrecht, Duke of Teschen, was a prominent member of the Austrian Imperial House of Habsburg-Lorraine. He went on to be appointed commander in chief of the Austro-Hungarian Army at the outbreak of World War I.

special exhibition the next morning. His Highness arrived somewhat in advance of Colonel Cody, and when they brought the buckers into the arena he insisted on remaining there also. The first mount made a dash directly toward His Highness, and but for the fact that Bill Langdon risked his own life by jumping in and pulling the duke out of the way, he doubtless would have been killed. This same old grand duke visited with Colonel Cody several times while we were in Vienna. He recalled the above circumstance of his former visit, adding that he was a skeptic no longer.

The Prater, where our tents were pitched in Vienna, is the playground of the big city—a veritable Coney Island. There were parks, gardens, theatres, circuses—in fact, everything in the way of Summer amusement, in full blast.

Within two minutes from our main entrance you could take a trip to heaven, hell, the North Pole, or any old place, for four cents. As ours was the "big show," everything was proclaimed American. There was even "American sourkrout" and "American beer." But the funniest, or rather most ridiculous thing I saw there, was an alleged American flag displayed at one of these "joints." It had four white and brownish-red stripes, with seven eight-pointed white stars on a green field.

June 15 we made a run South, of one hundred and seventy-five miles, to Budapest, capital of Hungary, a fine city of 800,000, on the Danube. The city takes its name from Buda and Pest, which are now united by

31. *The Royal Family's Visit to the Wild West at Rome, Italy, 1906.*

ten of the handsomest bridges in the world. Hungary is noted for its carriage and racing horses, and Budapest is one of the greatest horse markets in Europe. It was therefore but natural that the people should take a great interest in the Wild West, and, although every stitch of canvas was spread and every inch of seat plank in place, our enormous seating capacity was taxed to the utmost. While the entire programme was well received, Colonel Cody's shooting on horseback, the bucking horses, Johnny Baker's shooting act, the "Horse Fair," introducing our 200 magnificent draught horses; the Devlin Zouaves and the Arab Troupe met with special favor. Eight days were not long enough for Budapest, as thousands of people, many coming

from a distance, were unable to gain admission.
From Budapest we made a month of one day stands in Hungary. I am sorry to say that business was not up to our former standard. Hungary is purely an agricultural country, their methods of harvesting primitive, and a majority of the population, both men and women, were in the fields at the time we were there.
At Bekesaba,[14] July 2, the order of "Tigers" visited the grave of Henry Clark,[15] who was buried there in May, 1901, by the "Tigers" of the Barnum & Bailey Show. Speeches were made, and Prof. Sweeney's Cowboy Band rendered appropriate selections. To illustrate the friendly feelings that the Hungarians entertain for a stranger, I will mention the fact that Mr. Clark died just before the show's departure, and one man was left behind to attend the burial. He was assisted in every way by the natives, and five hundred school children followed poor Clark's body to its last resting place. The burial lot was purchased by the "Tigers," who also placed an appropriate monument over the grave.
We celebrated our fourth Fourth of July in foreign lands at Szeged, Hungary. The front of the show was artistically decorated in red, white and blue, Caterer Ballard gave us a fine dinner, the bands rendered good old Yankee airs, and we almost felt as if we were at home rather than on the frontier of Europe and Asia.

14. Currently Békéscsaba, Hungary.
15. Henry Clark was a member of the Railway Department of Barnum and Bailey's Circus. He died in an accident during the company's European tour.

We showed all the outposts of Eastern Europe along the borders of Turkey, Bulgaria, Romania, Serbia and Russia. We certainly had our troubles with interpreters. Some towns would be about equally divided between four or five nationalities, and, although they all understood German, the official language, each would insist on being addressed in his native language. We think we have a race problem in America, but it is more complicated and acute in Eastern Europe, and it is not a matter of color, either. The majority of the peasantry are on a par, educationally, with the negroes of our Southern States, and the poor Jew is far more persecuted. The stores and shops illustrate their wares on their signboards, because the majority of the population cannot read. Krakau,[16] Lemberg[17] and all towns along the Russian border were particularly lawless. They seemed to be a lot of natural born agitators.

Our first stand in the great German Empire was at Zitau, Saxony, August 15. For the three months preceding this date we had a multiplicity of languages to contend with, viz.: Hungarian, German, Slavonic, Romanian, Czech, Serbian, Polish, etc., and it certainly seemed good to get into a country where a universal language was spoken.

We played an unusually successful four days' engagement at Dresden, the capital of Saxony. Although we had rain every day, we turned people away at every

16. Currently Kraków, Poland, which the Wild West visited on August 4–5, 1906.
17. Currently Lviv, Ukraine, which the Wild West visited on July 28–30, 1906.

performance except one. I never saw so many people on a show ground in my life as there were at Dresden, Sunday afternoon, August 19. Although our seating capacity was about 17,000 people, we could not accommodate half of those who desired admission. There is a large colony of English and Americans at Dresden, who support a very respectable English daily newspaper. Governor Francis[18] and family, of Missouri, visited with Colonel Cody while we were at Dresden.

About this time our closing date, September 21, was announced, and we all began to prepare for it. The Indians were particularly active in buying clothes and valises—made in Germany. The cow punchers also put on European "togs," which so changed their personal appearance that one scarcely knew the other, and we all had to get acquainted over again.

We were at Plauen August 24, where we encountered regulation German business—the very best.

At Weimar, August 26, Colonel Cody received a telegram from the Grand Duke of Saxe-Weimar,[19] who regretted his absence from home, and his consequent inability to visit the Wild West, but the following day His Highness and party came over from Weisbaden

18. Democrat David Rowland Francis had served as mayor of St. Louis from 1885 to 1889 and as governor of Missouri from 1889 to 1893. Francis went on to be the last U.S. Ambassador to the Russian Empire (1916–1917). On Francis's fascinating political career see Barnes (2001).

19. William Ernest Charles Alexander Frederick Henry Bernard Albert George Herman was Grand Duke of Saxe-Weimar-Eisenach from 1901 until the dissolution of the German monarchies at the end of the World War I in 1918. He was therefore the last holder of the title.

32. The sideshow, 1906.

in motor cars. Colonel Cody also received royalty at Gera.[20]

United States Consul Harris,[21] at Chemnitz, was born in the same county in Iowa where Colonel Cody first saw the light of day, and he and his family were made a part of our troupe while we were at Chemnitz.

At Eisenach, August 27, the home of Martin Luther, the Reformer, the citadel was visited by a number of our boys.

Fulda, Prussia, where we stopped August 28, is only a small town of 20,000 population, but we had a fair afternoon and good night attendance.

---

20. Prince Heinrich XXIV of Reuss and his family attended the Wild West's performance in Gera on August 25, 1906.
21. Ernest Lloyd Harris was the U.S. Consul based at Chemnitz in 1905 and 1906.

At Hanau, August 29, we exhibited on one of Napoleon's historic battlefields.[22]

We had our first view of the Rhine at Worms. While it is a magnificent stream, it does not, in my opinion, possess the natural beauty of our great Mississippi or Hudson Rivers. While the Germans take every advantage of their natural resources, we, as a nation, have been sadly neglectful of them, especially as to our inland waterways.

August 31 found us at Saarbrucken, a city of 244,000 population, on the Saar River, with the city of St. Johann, 440,000, on the other side.

September 1 and 2 we had four big houses at Metz, Alsace-Lorraine (58,000 population), which was surrendered to Germany by the French in 1871. Although under the German government, it is still a French city, to all outward appearances.[23]

September 3 we were at the little principality of Luxembourg, where four kinds of money circulate, viz.: Luxembourg, German, French and Belgian.

At Bonn, September 6, we were visited by the Princess Victoria of Prussia,[24] youngest sister of the Kaiser, and a niece of King Edward VII of England. During

---

22. The French Army of Emperor Napoleon I (Bonaparte) defeated an Austrian and Bavarian force commanded by Karl Philipp von Wrede on October 30–31, 1813, at Hanau.

23. Metz was returned to France by the 1919 Treaty of Versailles.

24. Princess Victoria of Prussia was the daughter of Frederick III of Germany and thereby the sister of the reigning kaiser in 1906, Wilhelm II, and the granddaughter of Queen Victoria, her mother having been Victoria's eldest daughter, the Princess Victoria. Princess Victoria was therefore the niece of the reigning British monarch, Edward VII, as described by Griffin.

33. Sioux Indians, and Johnny Baker and Dollie, the Laughing horse.

the morning she paid a personal visit to Colonel Cody, who gallantly escorted her through the camp.

We made our last stand in the great German Empire at Munich-Gladbach,[25] September 8 and 9, to capacity business at every performance. We found Germany to be a well governed country, and well disposed towards the big American show.

We jumped into Belgium at Verviers, September 10, where our reception was all that could be desired, from every standpoint. In fact, it seemed like home to get back where French was spoken. I believe this is the only country, except China, where the "coin of the realm" has a hole in it. Their one and two cent nickel pieces have a round hole through the centre. Belgium is the most densely populated country in all Europe. Area, 11,373 square miles; population, six and one-half millions.

At Namur, September 11, we did a fine day's business on a very dusty lot.

Charleroi, where we exhibited September 12, is a big iron and steel town much like our own Charleroi in Pennsylvania. It was a "cracker jack," to use one of Colonel Cody's expressions—one of the banner stands of the season. The police were mounted on horseback, and had to keep on the move around the tents to keep the disappointed thousands, unable to gain admission at the doors, from going under the side walls.

We stopped one day at Mons, September 13, to good business.

25. Currently Mönchengladbach.

34. Opening day in Genoa (*top*) and double-deck tramcar used in England.

September 14 we invaded Brussels, the Belgian capital, for a four days' stay, and, although it rained torrents every day, we did capacity business with a full spread of canvas and all the seats up. Bruxelles (French) is a bright and gay cosmopolitan city of 531,000 people, aptly named "Petite Paris," as it seems to be entirely given up to pleasure. Everybody was apparently having a good time there. The *cafés* are as popular there as in Paris, the men being especially fond of them, and sit for hours at the little round tables drinking absinthe, wine, coffee or cognac. They spend their time at these *cafés* instead of being at work, and allow their poor, hard-working little wives to slave their lives away in keeping a grocery, or a laundry, or some such place.

From Brussels we went to Antwerp (Anvers), the business metropolis of Belgium, where we remained two days, September 18, 19. We had fine weather and did a big business both days. It was amusing to see the beggars of Antwerp make a dash for us when we left the cars, but they soon awoke to the fact that we were not tourists. The red guide-book seems to be a signal to the beggars for an onslaught, and they will follow the poor inoffensive tourists about, weeping and wailing, until they are literally forced to give them a few *sous*[26] in sheer desperation. It is said there are more street beggars in Antwerp than in any European city, outside of Spain and Italy.

From Antwerp we moved to the old fashioned

---

26. The *sou* was a low-value copper coin.

town of Ghent, in Flanders (population, 180,000). We gave two performances there September 20, and one performance afternoon of 21, which closed the season of 1906. While we had many struggles and hardships during the season, all obstacles were overcome by Manager Fred B. Hutchinson and his efficient staff. Take it all in all, the tour was a most successful one, both financially and artistically.

Colonel Cody, Jule Keene and family, Major John M. Burke and the Indians sailed for America on the S. S. Zealand, from Antwerp, September 22. Bill McCune, the Mexicans, Prof. Sweeney's Cowboy Band, and the balance of the American contingent sailed from Southampton, England, on the Philadelphia, the same date. All of the broncos, except the buckers and a few culled from the draught stock, were sold in a bunch to a Brussels firm, who sold them at auction in Ghent. The cars and wagons were shipped to the Barnum & Bailey[27] Winter quarters at Stoke-on-Trent, and the balance of the stock and Wild West paraphernalia were shipped by the Atlantic Transport Line to New York.

---

27. [Griffin note] In December, 1907, the Ringling Bros. acquired, by purchase, all the rights, titles and interests of the Barnum & Bailey, Ltd., which was an English syndicate. This makes the five Ringlings, viz., Al., Otto, John, Charlie and Alf. T., the most extensive owners of show property in the world—the Ringling Bros.' World's Greatest Shows, Barnum & Bailey's Greatest Show on Earth and the Adam Forepaugh & Sells Bros.' Combined Shows, comprising the three biggest shows in the world, excepting, of course, Buffalo Bill's Wild West.

CHAPTER IX—1906–1907

Closing of the Tour—Departure for and Arrival at New York—Impressions of New York After Four Years Abroad

The last of our four years abroad (1906), during which we encountered sixteen different languages, was a particularly trying one. When we closed our season at Ghent, Belgium, afternoon of September 21, I felt as though I was on the verge of nervous prostration, having been at a high nervous tension all Summer, as a result of the constant effort to understand and make myself understood in so many foreign lands.

As soon as the strain was off it seemed as though I would collapse if I did not get away from it. Therefore I hied myself to London as soon as possible.

After listening to polyglot languages for two years, it seemed so strange to hear nothing but our native tongue.

While walking in the streets of London we would involuntarily turn around and stare at people merely because they were talking English.

On October 13 we embarked on the good ship Lucania, Cunard Line, for America, and after a pleasant voyage of six days and a few hours, landed at New York October 20.

I had heard so much of the exactions of the American

custom officials, that I felt greatly relieved when the ordeal was over. For my part I cannot see where they are any more severe than in other countries.

In "little old New York" once more, I could quickly see a change in the conditions of four years ago. In the first place I never saw the streets in such bad condition as they are now—a result of the great activity in building. The Flatiron and Times Building were new to me, and it made my neck stiff trying to look up to the top. A trip down lower Broadway, among the skyscrapers, reminded me of going up the Royal Gorge towards Leadville. The subway had been completed during my absence, and after riding in the old District Underground Railway and "Tuppenny Tube" of London, and the Metropolitan Underground Railway of Paris, I unhesitatingly pronounce the New York subway the most perfect in the world, with the "Tuppenny Tube," of Central London, a close second.

The great bandwagon-like touring cars, or rubberneck wagons, were also something I had never seen before, and it struck me as being a cheap and efficient way of seeing the sights of the city. They start from most of the prominent hotels every hour, with a guide who points out the principal objects of interest on the route, and the fare is only one dollar for the trip.

When I left America, four years ago, the souvenir postcard craze had not yet struck New York, but upon my arrival in England, I found it was all the rage there. Upon my return to New York I found the disease, after a careful diagnosis, to be far more acute than it ever was in Europe.

During my absence abroad I had heard and read a great deal about the New York Hippodrome, and while its immense proportions came up to my expectations, I was disappointed in the spectacle, "A Society Circus." I have since seen at this establishment two grand bills—"Pioneer Days" and "Neptune's Daughter," and "Sporting Days" and "The Battle of the Skies"—which, for general grandeur, mysterious effects, feminine beauty and scenic splendor, excel anything of the kind that I saw in all Europe.

The songs were all new and the vaudeville situation revolutionized, inasmuch as most of the vaudeville theatres had been doing their own booking, while now the bookings are in the hands of the agents, this custom prevailing also in Europe—Tony Pastor[1] being a notable exception to the above rule.

The numerous penny arcades and moving picture shows scattered all over the city were another new wrinkle in American showmanship, and the great business they were all doing demonstrated that it was indeed a long felt want—cheap, popular and innocent amusement for the masses.

The people are more polite in Europe than in America. In England everything is "'if you please"; France, "s'il vous plait"[2]; Germany and Austria, "bitte

---

1. Tony Pastor was a former circus ringmaster who moved into theater management in the 1880s in New York. His introduction of polite variety programs is generally recognized as being a crucial step in the development of vaudeville. Pastor's reminiscences on the early days of vaudeville were published in an interview in the *New York Times* on April 21, 1907.

2. French for "please."

schön"[3]; Hungary, "Tessék"[4]; Italy, "grazie"[5]; etc.—all very polite. Well, you know how it is here; there is at least room for improvement.

I also noticed what I never knew before—that Americans are more given to the use of slang than any other nation in the world, and that the slang expressions most in vogue four years ago are now almost obsolete, while other *bon mots*[6] have been coined to take their place.

"Benzine buggy,"[7] "skidoo,"[8] "twenty-three"[9] and "lemon"[10] were all as incomprehensible to me as so much Chinese.

But these were only impressions of New York City, which is not America any more than London is England or Paris is France.

The End

---

3. German for "you're welcome."
4. A Hungarian word for "please" when offering something.
5. Italian for "thank you."
6. French for "good words" used here in the sense of "turns of phrase."
7. An automobile.
8. A variation of "skedaddle," meaning to go away.
9. A term for a telegraph message of extreme urgency.
10. A flop or failure.

OFFICIAL ROSTER OF BUFFALO BILL'S WILD WEST

Season of 1907

U.S.A.

Cody & Bailey	Owners
Fred Bailey Hutchinson	Manager
Louis E. Cook	General Agent
M. Coyle	R. R. Contractor
Major John M. Burke	Press Agent in Advance
Walter K. Hill	Press Agent in Advance
S. H. (Pop) Semon	Contracting Agent
D. F. Lynch	Contracting Agent
E. H. Wood	Agent Advertising Car No. 1
D. De Baugh	Agent Advertising Car No. 2
W. Ford	Agent Advertising Car No. 3
Chas. Meredith	Special Agent
Thomas Clare	Twenty-four Hour Agent
S. H. Fielder	Twenty-four Hour Agent
L. Monterey	Inspector of Advertising
F. W. Hall	Press Agent With Show
T. L. Evans	Head of Financial Department
Joe Bailey Harper	Treasurer
Reginald Whitehead	Chartered Accountant
Charles Mercer	Secretary
Johnny Baker	Arenic Director

Matt Sanders . . . . .Master of Properties
Cy Compton . . . . Chief of Cowboys
Thomas Rankine . . . . Principal Announcer
Wm. Sweeney. . . . . Bandmaster
Jacob Posey. . . . . Master of Stock
Jacob Platt. . . . . Superintendent of Canvas
D. Ballard . . . . Caterer
Thomas Tune . . . . Chef
Peter Halstead . . . . Master Mechanic
Col. Chas. Seely . . . . Legal Adjuster
R. P. Murphy. . . . . Master Transportation
John Eberle . . . . General Superintendent

TICKET SELLERS

White Wagon, Reserves—O. S. Demske and John Hammel; *Red Wagon, General Admission*—Ben (Blondy) Powell and Karl E. Grigsby; *Blue Wagon, General Admission*—Nate Davis and Bill Cloud.

TICKET TAKERS

Carlo Ratte, Robert Coverdale, Frank Quinn, Wm. Boyd, Frank McKay.

SIDE SHOW

Chas. E. Griffin, Manager; Paul J. Staunton, Principal Orator; Fred I. Griffin, Assistant Orator and Ticket Seller; C. F. Mack, Ticket Seller and Punch and Judy; John Lovely and H. E. Tudor, Ticket Takers; Octavia, Snake Charmer; Griffin, the Yankee Yogi, conjuror; Fred Walters, Blue Man; Lentini, Three-Legged Man; Jessica, Moss Haired Lady; Harry Wilson and Harry Keigel, Tattooed Men; Grace Gilbert, Auburn Bearded Venus; Marvelous Mandy, Man With Iron

Skull; Miss Anna, Physical Culture Girl; Sig. Sagatta's Belgian Hare Band; J. D. Cramer, Elastic Skin and Giraffe Neck; Julia Griffin, Mind Reader; C. A. Bonney, Scotch Piper and Polyphonist; Mlle. Equinas, Parisian Horse Lady; Balbroma, High Priest of the Fire Worshippers; Prof. James T. Jukes, one of the Original P. T. Barnum Bohemian Glass Blowers; Tito Altobelli's Italian Band; Monroe Sisters, Musical Artists; Horace E. Tudor, Master of Side Show Canvas.

CONCERT

Chas. E. Griffin, Manager; Togo and Sarbro, Japanese Jugglers; Clymer, Allen and Monroe Sisters, Musical Act; Julia Arcaris, Song and Dance; James and Celia Welch, Comedy Sketch Artists; Major Kelleher, Drum Major; Miss Daly, Vocalist; Boyd and Lovely, Eccentric Comedians; James Rutherford, Monologue.

CANDY STANDS

Walter Beckwith, Superintendent; C. Zelno, "Babe" Ramsay, Assistants.

PROGRAMS

Joseph Meyer, 27 East Twenty-second Street, New York, Lessee; Tom Burke, in Charge.

MYTHOPLASM
(MOVING PICTURE SHOW IN BLACK TENT)

Al. Conlon, Manager; Clarence Wright, Electrician.

LIGHTS (BOLTE & WEYER SYSTEM)

Pete Walker, Superintendent.

PINKERTON DETECTIVE

J. Garner.

CHIEF USHERS
Wm. McCune and Archie Daly.

CHIEF PORTER
Charles Carroll.

PROGRAMME OF BUFFALO BILL'S WILD WEST

Season of 1907

U.S.A.

1. OVERTURE. "Star Spangled Banner"—Cowboy Band, Wm. Sweeney, Leader.

2. GRAND REVIEW. Introducing Rough Riders of the World, genuine Sioux and Cheyenne Indians, Cowboys, Cossacks, Mexicans, Scouts and Guides, veteran members of the United States Cavalry, a group of Western Girl Rough Riders, and a detachment of colorguards, soldiers of the armies of America, England, Germany, Japan, Russia, Arabia and Mexico.

3. RACE OF RACES. Race between a Cowboy, Cossack, Mexican, Arab and Indian, on Mexican, Bronco, Indian and Arabian horses. Attention is directed to the different seats in saddle by the various riders.

4. U.S. ARTILLERY DRILL. Showing the old muzzle-loading methods. The guns used are relics of the Civil War.

5. PONY EXPRESS. A former Pony Express rider will show how telegrams of the Republic were distributed and carried across the continent previous to the building of telegraphs and railways.

6. EMIGRANT TRAIN. Illustrating a prairie Emigrant Train crossing the plains. It is attacked by marauding Indians, and they are repulsed by the scouts and cowboys. While in camp there will be a quadrille on horseback, and other camp-fire amusements.

7. ARABS AND JAPANESE. In various feats of agility.

8. AN ATTACK ON THE DEADWOOD STAGECOACH BY INDIANS. Repulse of the Indians and rescue of the stage, passengers and mail, by cowboys and scouts.

9. COL. W. F. CODY. The original Buffalo Bill, the last of the great scouts; the first to conceive, originate and produce this class of realistic entertainment. He will give an exhibition of expert shooting from horseback, while galloping around the arena.

10. THE BATTLE OF SUMMIT SPRINGS. One of the deciding conflicts in Indian warfare was fought on July 11, 1869, in Eastern Colorado, near the border line of Nebraska. The command was composed of the Fifth United States Cavalry and Pawnee scouts, under the command of Gen. E. A. Carr, of the United States Army. Buffalo Bill was chief of General Carr's scouts and guides. The Indians were renegades from the tribes of Sioux, Cheyennes and Arapahoes, banded together under the leadership of Tall Bull, and were known as "The Dog Soldiers." These Indians had been murdering and committing depredations on the borders of Kansas and Nebraska, and this command had been sent to discover and annihilate them if possible. After several days' scouting, Buffalo Bill found the Indian trail, which the command at once followed, and after continuing

for more than two hundred miles, Buffalo Bill located the Indian camp, and in a spirited assault the forces under General Carr completely routed Tall Bull and his "Dog Soldiers," capturing the entire village, killing many of the warriors and capturing the Indian women and children. They also rescued two white women which the Indians held as prisoners. During the engagement Buffalo Bill shot and killed the Indian chief, Tall Bull.

11. DEVLIN ZOUAVES. In manual of arms, lightning drills, finishing with an exhibition of wall-scaling, showing the adaptability of citizen-soldiery in warfare.

12. A GROUP OF AMERICANS from Old Mexico, Illustrating the use of the lasso.

13. VETERANS FROM THE SIXTH United States Cavalry in military exercises and exhibitions of athletic sports and horsemanship on Western range horses.

14. JOHNNY BAKER. The celebrated American Marksman.

15. THE GREAT TRAIN HOLD-UP AND BANDIT HUNTERS OF THE UNION PACIFIC will be a scene representing a train hold-up in the Western wilds. The bandits stop the train, uncouple the engine from the coaches, rob the express car and blow open the safe. Meanwhile the passengers are lined up and despoiled of their valuables. The scene ends with the arrival of the Bandit Hunters of the Union Pacific, who capture or kill the robbers.

16. INDIAN BOYS' RACE. Racing by Indian boys on bareback ponies.

17. COWBOYS' FUN. Picking objects from the ground, lassoing, and riding wild horses.

18. COSSACKS FROM THE CAUCASUS OF RUSSIA In feats of horsemanship.

19. A HOLIDAY AT "T-E" RANCH IN WYOMING. The final number on our programme will be a holiday at "T-E" Ranch, the home of Buffalo Bill. The frontiersmen and cowboys have assembled for an afternoon of pleasure. The arrival of the mail-carrier, which is always an important event, and a troop of range horses in high school acts. The festivities are interrupted by an attack on the ranch by a band of Indians, and they are repulsed by the cowboys, the scene of present happy ranch home life is transposed into one of the old, strenuous days by dramatic license, to form a climax to the ending of the exhibition, permitting the red and the white men to line up in compact, friendly mass, to effectively give the audience a FINAL SALUTE.

APPENDIX

Buffalo Bill's Wild West in Europe, 1902–1906

1902

December 6–31, 1902 London, England

1903

January 1, 1903–April 4, 1903 London, England
April 13, 1903–May 2, 1903 Manchester, England
May 5–23, 1903 Liverpool, England
May 25, 1903 Warrington, England
May 26, 1903 Birkenhead, England
May 27, 1903 Rhyl, Wales
May 28, 1903 Bangor, Wales
May 29, 1903 Ruabon, Wales
May 30, 1903 Shrewsbury, England
June 1–13, 1903 Birmingham, England
June 15, 1903 Worcester, England
June 16, 1903 Kidderminster, England
June 17, 1903 Dudley, England
June 18, 1903 Wolverhampton, England
June 19, 1903 Stafford, England
June 20, 1903 Coventry, England
June 22, 1903 Rugby, England
June 23, 1903 Leamington, England

June 24, 1903 Banbury, England
June 25, 1903 Oxford, England
June 26–27, 1903 Reading, England
June 29, 1903 Swindon, England
June 30, 1903 Cheltenham, England
July 1, 1903 Gloucester, England
July 2, 1903 Hereford, England
July 3, 1903 Abergavenny, Wales
July 6–11, 1903 Cardiff, Wales
July 13, 1903 Llanelli, Wales
July 14–15, 1903 Swansea, Wales
July 16, 1903 Newport, Wales
July 17, 1903 Bath, England
July 18, 1903 Weston-super-Mare, England
July 20–23, 1903 Bristol, England
July 24, 1903 Westbury, England
July 25, 1903 Yeovil, England
July 27, 1903 Barnstaple, England
July 28, 1903 Exeter, England
July 29, 1903 Newton Abbot, England
July 30, 1903–August 1, 1903 Plymouth, England
August 3, 1903 Taunton, England
August 4, 1903 Weymouth, England
August 5, 1903 Bournemouth, England
August 6, 1903 Salisbury, England
August 7–8, 1903 Southampton, England
August 10–12, 1903 Portsmouth, England
August 13–15, 1903 Brighton, England
August 17, 1903 Guildford, England
August 18, 1903 Tunbridge Wells, England

August 19, 1903   Eastbourne, England
August 20, 1903   Hastings, England
August 21, 1903   Ashford, England
August 22, 1903   Folkestone, England
August 24, 1903   Ramsgate, England
August 25, 1903   Margate, England
August 26, 1903   Canterbury, England
August 27, 1903   Maidstone, England
August 28, 1903   Chatham, England
August 29, 1903   Croydon, England
August 31, 1903   Watford, England
September 1, 1903   Luton, England
September 2, 1903   Leyton, England
September 3, 1903   Southend, England
September 4, 1903   Colchester, England
September 5, 1903   Bury St. Edmonds, England
September 7, 1903   Ipswich, England
September 8, 1903   Lowestoft, England
September 9, 1903   Great Yarmouth, England
September 10, 1903   Norwich, England
September 11, 1903   King's Lynn, England
September 12, 1903   Wisbech, England
September 14, 1903   Peterborough, England
September 15, 1903   Ely, England
September 16, 1903   Bedford, England
September 17, 1903   Northampton, England
September 18, 1903   Wellingborough, England
September 19, 1903   Kettering, England
September 21–22, 1903   Leicester, England
September 23, 1903   Spalding, England

September 24, 1903   Boston, England
September 25, 1903   Grantham, England
September 26, 1903   Lincoln, England
September 28, 1903–October 3, 1903   Leeds, England
October 5–6, 1903   Bradford, England
October 7, 1903   Keighley, England
October 8, 1903   Halifax, England
October 9, 1903   Wakefield, England
October 10, 1903   Doncaster, England
October 12–15, 1903   Sheffield, England
October 16–17, 1903   Chesterfield, England
October 19–20, 1903   Nottingham, England
October 21, 1903   Loughborough, England
October 22, 1903   Derby, England
October 23, 1903   Burton, England

1904

April 25, 1904   Stoke-on-Trent, England
April 26, 1904   Nuneaton, England
April 27, 1904   Walsall, England
April 28, 1904   Stourbridge, England
April 29, 1904   Wellington, England
April 30, 1904   Crewe, England
May 2, 1904   Llandudno, Wales
May 3, 1904   Holyhead, Wales
May 4, 1904   Carnarvon, Wales
May 5, 1904   Portmadoc, Wales
May 6, 1904   Dolgelly, Wales
May 7, 1904   Aberystwyth, Wales
May 9, 1904   Chester, England

May 10, 1904	Wrexham, Wales
May 11, 1904	Oswestry, Wales
May 12, 1904	Builth Wells, Wales
May 13, 1904	Carmarthen, Wales
May 14, 1904	Pembroke Dock, Wales
May 16, 1904	Llanelli, Wales
May 17, 1904	Neath, Wales
May 18, 1904	Bridgend, Wales
May 19, 1904	Barry Dock, Wales
May 20-21, 1904	Cardiff, Wales
May 23, 1904	Stroud, England
May 24, 1904	Trowbridge, England
May 25, 1904	Wells, Somerset, England
May 26 1904	Bridgewater, England
May 27, 1904	Exmouth, England
May 28, 1904	Torquay, England
May 30, 1904	Penzance, England
May 31, 1904	Cambourne, England
June 1, 1904	Truro, England
June 2, 1904	Bodmin, England
June 3, 1904	Plymouth, England
June 4, 1904	Taunton, England
June 6, 1904	Dorchester, England
June 7, 1904	Poole, England
June 8, 1904	Southampton, England
June 9, 1904	Winchester, England
June 10, 1904	Newbury, England
June 11, 1904	High Wycombe, England
June 13, 1904	Windsor, England
June 14, 1904	Aldershot, England

June 15, 1904　　Horsham, England
June 16, 1904　　Lewes, Sussex, England
June 17, 1904　　Redhill, Surrey, England
June 18, 1904　　Wimbledon, England
June 20, 1904　　Chelmsford, England
June 21, 1904　　Ilford, England
June 22, 1904　　St. Albans, England
June 23, 1904　　Hitchin, England
June 24, 1904　　Cambridge, England
June 25, 1904　　Ilkeston, England
June 27, 1904　　Mansfield, England
June 28, 1904　　Rotherham, England
June 29, 1904　　Gainsborough, England
June 30, 1904　　Great Grimsby, England
July 1–2, 1904　　Hull, England
July 4, 1904　　York, England
July 5, 1904　　Scarborough, England
July 6, 1904　　Darlington, England
July 7, 1904　　Stockton-on-Tees, England
July 8, 1904　　Middlesbrough, England
July 9, 1904　　West Hartlepool, England
July 11–16, 1904　　Newcastle-on-Tyne, England
July 18–19, 1904　　Sunderland, England
July 20, 1904　　Durham, England
July 21, 1904　　South Shields, England
July 22, 1904　　Hexham, England
July 23, 1904　　North Shields, England
July 25, 1904　　Berwick-upon-Tweed, England
July 26, 1904　　Hawick, Scotland
July 27, 1904　　Galashiels, Scotland

July 28, 1904   Motherwell, Scotland
July 29, 1904   Coatbridge, Scotland
July 30, 1904   Dumbarton, Scotland
August 1–6, 1904   Glasgow, Scotland
August 8–13, 1904   Edinburgh, Scotland
August 15, 1904   Falkirk, Scotland
August 16, 1904   Dunfermline, Scotland
August 17, 1904   Kirkcaldy, Scotland
August 18–20, 1904   Dundee, Scotland
August 22, 1904   Arbroath, Scotland
August 23, 1904   Forfar, Scotland
August 24, 1904   Montrose, Scotland
August 25–27, 1904   Aberdeen, Scotland
August 29, 1904   Peterhead, Scotland
August 30, 1904   Fraserburgh, Scotland
August 31, 1904   Huntly, Scotland
September 1, 1904   Elgin, Scotland
September 2–3, 1904   Inverness, Scotland
September 5, 1904   Perth, Scotland
September 6, 1904   Stirling, Scotland
September 7, 1904   Paisley, Scotland
September 8, 1904   Greenock, Scotland
September 9, 1904   Saltcoats, Scotland
September 10, 1904   Kilmarnock, Scotland
September 12, 1904   Ayr, Scotland
September 13, 1904   Stranraer, Scotland
September 14, 1904   Dumfries, Scotland
September 15, 1904   Carlisle, England
September 16, 1904   Penrith, England
September 17, 1904   Maryport, England

September 19, 1904   Wokingham, England
September 20, 1904   Whitehaven, England
September 21, 1904   Barrow-in-Furness, England
September 22, 1904   Kendal, England
September 23, 1904   Lancaster, England
September 24, 1904   Blackpool, England
September 26, 1904   Preston, England
September 27, 1904   Blackburn, England
September 28, 1904   Chorley, England
September 29, 1904   Wigan, England
September 30, 1904   Southport, England
October 1, 1904   St. Helens, England
October 2, 1904   Leigh, England
October 4, 1904   Bolton, England
October 5, 1904   Bury, England
October 6, 1904   Rochdale, England
October 7, 1904   Oldham, England
October 8, 1904   Burnley, England
October 10, 1904   Skipton, England
October 11, 1904   Harrogate, England
October 12, 1904   Castleford, England
October 13, 1904   Barnsley, England
October 14, 1904   Huddersfield, England
October 15, 1904   Ashton-under-Lyne, England
October 17, 1904   Glossop, England
October 18, 1904   Stockport, England
October 19, 1904   Northwick, England
October 20, 1904   Macclesfield, England
October 21, 1904   Hanley, England

1905

April 2, 1905–June 4, 1905   Paris, France
June 5, 1905   Chartres, France
June 6, 1905   Alençon, France
June 7, 1905   Fleurs, France
June 8, 1905   Saint-Lô, France
June 9, 1905   Cherbourg, France
June 10–11, 1905   Caen, France
June 12, 1905   Lisieux, France
June 13, 1905   Evreux, France
June 14, 1905   Elbeuf, France
June 15–16, 1905   Rouen, France
June 17–18, 1905   Le Havre, France
June 19, 1905   Dieppe, France
June 20, 1905   Abbeville, France
June 21–22, 1905   Amiens, France
June 23, 1905   Arras, France
June 24, 1905   Douai, France
June 25, 1905   Dunkirk, France
June 26, 1905   Calais, France
June 27, 1905   Boulogne, France
June 28, 1905   Armentières, France
June 29–30, 1905   Roubaix, France
July 1–4, 1905   Lille, France
July 5, 1905   Valenciennes, France
July 6, 1905   Maubeuge, France
July 7, 1905   Cambrai, France
July 8, 1905   Saint-Quentin, France
July 9, 1905   Compiègne, France
July 10, 1905   Laon, France

July 11–13, 1905   Reims, France
July 14, 1905   Mézières-Charleville, France
July 15, 1905   Sedan, France
July 16, 1905   Verdun, France
July 17, 1905   Chalon-sur-Marne, France
July 18, 1905   Bar-le-Duc, France
July 19–20, 1905   Nancy, France
July 21, 1905   Lunéville, France
July 22, 1905   Saint-Dié-des-Vosges, France
July 23, 1905   Epinal, France
July 24, 1905   Belfort, France
July 25, 1905   Vesoul, France
July 26, 1905   Chaumont, France
July 27, 1905   Troyes, France
July 28, 1905   Sens, France
July 29, 1905   Auxerre, France
July 30–31, 1905   Dijon, France
August 1, 1905   Besançon, France
August 2, 1905   Lons-le-Saunier, France
August 3, 1905   Bourg, France
August 4–13, 1905   Lyon, France
August 14, 1905   Mâcon, France
August 15, 1905   Chalon-sur-Saône, France
August 16, 1905   Le Creusot, France
August 17, 1905   Nevers, France
August 18, 1905   Moulins-sur-Allier, France
August 19, 1905   Roanne, France
August 20, 1905   Vichy, France
August 21, 1905   Riom, France
August 22, 1905   Montluçon, France

August 23, 1905   Bourges, France
August 24–25, 1905   Orléans, France
August 26, 1905   Saumur, France
August 27, 1905   Angers, France
August 29, 1905   Cholet, France
August 30, 1905   Thouars, France
August 31, 1905   Châtellerault, France
September 1, 1905   Poitiers, France
September 2, 1905   Angoulême, France
September 3, 1905   Saintes, France
September 4, 1905   Rochefort, France
September 5, 1905   La Rochelle, France
September 6, 1905   Niort, France
September 7, 1905   La-Roche-sur-Yon, France
September 8, 1905   Saint-Nazaire, France
September 9, 1905   Vannes, France
September 10, 1905   Lorient, France
September 11, 1905   Quimper, France
September 12, 1905   Brest, France
September 13, 1905   Saint-Brieuc, France
September 14, 1905   Saint-Malo, France
September 15, 1905   Rennes, France
September 16, 1905   Laval, France
September 17, 1905   Le Mans, France
September 18, 1905   Tours, France
September 19, 1905   Châteauroux, France
September 20, 1905   Limoges, France
September 21, 1905   Périgueux, France
September 22, 1905-October 1, 1905   Bordeaux, France
October 2, 1905   Dax, France

October 3, 1905　Bayonne, France
October 4, 1905　Pau, France
October 5, 1905　Tarbes, France
October 6, 1905　Mont-de-Marsan, France
October 7, 1905　Agen, France
October 8, 1905　Villeneuve-sur-Lot, France
October 9, 1905　Bergerac, France
October 10, 1905　Brive-la-Gaillarde, France
October 11, 1905　Cahors, France
October 12, 1905　Montauban, France
October 13–15, 1905　Toulouse, France
October 16, 1905　Albi, France
October 17, 1905　Castres, France
October 18, 1905　Carcassonne, France
October 19, 1905　Narbonne, France
October 20, 1905　Perpignan, France
October 21–22, 1905　Béziers, France
October 23, 1905　Sète, France
October 24–25, 1905　Montpellier, France
October 26, 1905　Alès, France
October 27–28, 1905　Nîmes, France
October 29, 1905　Avignon, France
October 30, 1905　Arles, France
October 31, 1905　Aix, France
November 1, 1905–December 11, 1905　Marseille, France

1906

March 4–5, 1906　Marseille, France
March 6–7, 1906　Toulon, France
March 8, 1906　Draguignan, France

March 9–12, 1906   Nice, France
March 14–16, 1906   Genoa, Italy
March 17, 1906   La Spezia, Italy
March 18–20, 1906   Livorno, Italy
March 22–28, 1906   Rome, Italy
March 29, 1906   Terni, Italy
March 30, 1906   Perugia, Italy
March 31, 1906   Arezzo, Italy
April 1–3, 1906   Florence, Italy
April 4, 1906   Pisa, Italy
April 5, 1906   Parma, Italy
April 6–7, 1906   Modena, Italy
April 8, 1906   Bologna, Italy
April 9, 1906   Forlì, Italy
April 10, 1906   Ancona, Italy
April 11, 1906   Rimini, Italy
April 12, 1906   Ravenna, Italy
April 13, 1906   Ferrara, Italy
April 14, 1906   Padua, Italy
April 15–16, 1906   Verona, Italy
April 17, 1906   Mantua, Italy
April 18, 1906   Cremona, Italy
April 19, 1906   Piacenza, Italy
April 20, 1906   Pavia, Italy
April 21, 1906   Alessandria, Italy
April 22–26, 1906   Turin, Italy
April 27, 1906   Asti, Italy
April 28, 1906   Novara, Italy
April 29, 1906   Como, Italy
April 30, 1906–May 5, 1906   Milan, Italy

May 7, 1906 Bergamo, Italy
May 8, 1906 Brescia, Italy
May 9, 1906 Vicenza, Italy
May 10, 1906 Treviso, Italy
May 11, 1906 Udine, Italy
May 13–15, 1906 Trieste, Italy[1]
May 16, 1906 Ljubljana,[2] Slovenia
May 17–18, 1906 Zagreb,[3] Croatia
May 19, 1906 Maribor,[4] Slovenia
May 20, 1906 Klagenfurt, Austria
May 21–22, 1906 Graz, Austria
May 23, 1906 Lechen, Austria
May 24, 1906 Linz, Austria
May 26, 1906–June 14, 1906 Vienna, Austria
June 16–24, 1906 Budapest, Hungary
June 25, 1906 Miskolc, Hungary
June 26, 1906 Kosice,[5] Slovakia
June 27, 1906 Uzhhorod,[6] Ukraine
June 28, 1906 Mukacheve,[7] Ukraine
June 29, 1906 Nyíregyháza, Hungary
June 30, 1906–July 1, 1906 Debrecen, Hungary
July 2, 1906 Békéscsaba, Hungary
July 3, 1906 Szentes, Hungary
July 4, 1906 Szeged, Hungary
July 5, 1906 Kikinda,[8] Serbia
July 6, 1906 Zrenjanin,[9] Serbia
July 7, 1906 Pančevo,[10] Serbia
July 8, 1906 Vršac,[11] Serbia
July 9, 1906 Timişoara,[12] Romania
July 10–11, 1906 Arad, Romania

July 12, 1906   Alba Lulia,[13] Romania
July 13, 1906   Sibiu,[14] Romania
July 14–15, 1906   Braşov,[15] Romania
July 16, 1906   Sighişoara,[16] Romania
July 17, 1906   Târgu Mureş,[17] Romania
July 18–19, 1906   Cluj-Napoca,[18] Romania
July 20, 1906   Oradea,[19] Romania
July 21, 1906   Satu Mare,[20] Romania
July 22, 1906   Sighetu Marmaţiei,[21] Romania
July 23, 1906   Kolomyia, Ukraine
July 24–25, 1906   Chernovtsys,[22] Ukraine
July 26, 1906   Luano-Frankivsk,[23] Ukraine
July 27, 1906   Ternopil, Ukraine
July 28–30, 1906   Lviv,[24] Ukraine
August 1, 1906   Przemyśl, Poland
August 2, 1906   Rzeszów, Poland
August 3, 1906   Tarnów, Poland
August 4–5, 1906   Kraków, Poland
August 6, 1906   Bielsko-Biała,[25] Poland
August 7, 1906   Cieszyn,[26] Poland
August 8, 1906   Ostrava,[27] Czech Republic
August 9, 1906   Opava,[28] Czech Republic
August 10, 1906   Přerov,[29] Czech Republic
August 11–12, 1906   Brno,[30] Czech Republic
August 13, 1906   Jihlava,[31] Czech Republic
August 15, 1906   Zittau, Germany
August 16, 1906   Bautzen, Germany
August 17–20, 1906   Dresden, Germany
August 21–22, 1906   Chemnitz, Germany
August 23, 1906   Zwickau, Germany

August 24, 1906 Plauen, Germany
August 25, 1906 Gera, Germany
August 26, 1906 Weimar, Germany
August 27, 1906 Eisenach, Germany
August 28, 1906 Fulda, Germany
August 29, 1906 Hanau, Germany
August 30, 1906 Worms, Germany
August 31, 1906 Saarbrucken, Germany
September 1–2, 1906 Metz,[32] France
September 3, 1906 Luxemburg, Luxemburg
September 4, 1906 Trier, Germany
September 5, 1906 Coblenz, Germany
September 6, 1906 Bonn, Germany
September 7, 1906 Duren, Germany
September 8–9, 1906 Mönchengladbach, Germany
September 10, 1906 Verviers, Belgium
September 11, 1906 Namur, Belgium
September 12, 1906 Charleroi, Belgium
September 13, 1906 Mons, Belgium
September 14–17, 1906 Brussels, Belgium
September 18–19, 1906 Antwerp, Belgium
September 20–21, 1906 Ghent, Belgium

Notes

1. Between May 13 and August 13, 1906, the Wild West toured in what was then the Austro-Hungarian Empire. Current spellings of town names and states names are given. When substantial differences exist for the place names used at the time of the tour, the former names are given as notes.
2. Formerly Laibach.
3. Formerly Agram.

4. Formerly Marburg.
5. Formerly Kassa.
6. Formerly Ungvar.
7. Formerly Munkacs.
8. Formerly Nagy-Kikinda.
9. Formerly Nagy-Becskerck.
10. Formerly Pancsova.
11. Formerly Versecz.
12. Formerly Temesvar.
13. Formerly Gyula-Fehervar.
14. Formerly Nagyszeben.
15. Formerly Brasso.
16. Formerly Segesvar.
17. Formerly Mar-Vasarhely.
18. Formerly Kolozsvar.
19. Formerly Nagyvárad.
20. Formerly Szatamar-Nemeti.
21. Formerly Maramar-Sziget.
22. Formerly Czernowitz.
23. Formerly Stanislau.
24. Formerly Lemberg.
25. Formerly Biala.
26. Formerly Teschen.
27. Formerly Mahr-Ostrau.
28. Formerly Troppau.
29. Formerly Prerau.
30. Formerly Brunn.
31. Formerly Iglau.
32. In 1906 Metz was part of Germany.

BIBLIOGRAPHY

Adams, Bluford. *E Pluribus Barnum: The Great Showman and the Making of U.S. Popular Culture*. Minneapolis: University of Minnesota Press, 1997.

Assael, Brenda. *The Circus and Victorian Society*. Charlottesville: University of Virginia Press, 2005.

Barnes, Harper. *Standing on a Volcano: The Life and Times of David Rowland Francis*. St Louis: Missouri Historical Society, 2001.

Blair, John G. "Blackface Minstrels and *Buffalo Bill's Wild West*: Nineteenth-Century Entertainment Forms as Cultural Exports." In *European Readings of American Popular Culture: Contributions to the Study of Popular Culture, Number 50*, edited by John Dean and Jean-Paul Gabillet, 3–12. Westport CT: Greenwood, 1996.

Bostock, Frank C. *The Training of Wild Animals*. Amsterdam: Fredonia, 2003.

Bredin, Jean-Denis. *The Affair: The Case of Alfred Dreyfus*. New York: George Braziller, 1986.

Bridger, Bobby. *Buffalo Bill and Sitting Bull: Inventing the Wild West*. Austin: University of Texas Press, 2002.

Carter, Robert A. *Buffalo Bill Cody: The Man Behind the Legend*. Edison NJ: Castle, 2005.

Cody, William F. *The Life of Hon. William F. Cody, Known as Buffalo Bill: The Famous Hunter, Scout and Guide. An Autobiography.* Foreword by Don Russell. Hartford CT: Frank E. Bliss, 1879; rpt. Lincoln: University of Nebraska Press, 1978.

Cunningham, Tom F. *"Your Fathers the Ghosts": Buffalo Bill's Wild West in Scotland.* Edinburgh: Black & White, 2007.

Dean, John, and Jean-Paul Gabillet, eds. *European Readings of American Popular Culture: Contributions to the Study of Popular Culture, No. 50.* Westport CT: Greenwood, 1996.

Feest, Christian F. *Indians and Europe.* Lincoln: University of Nebraska Press, 1999.

Fellows, Dexter W. *This Way to the Big Show: The Life of Dexter Fellows.* New York: Viking, 1936.

Fiorentino, Daniele. "'Those Red-Brick Faces': European Reactions to the Indians of Buffalo Bill's Wild West Show." In *Indians and Europe*, edited by Christian F. Feest, 403–15. Lincoln: University of Nebraska Press, 1999.

Franch, John. *Robber Baron: The Life of Charles Tyson Yerkes.* Champaign: University of Illinois Press, 2006.

Gallop, Alan. *Buffalo Bill's British Wild West.* Phoenix Mill, UK: Sutton, 2001.

Grant, H. Roger. "An Iowan with Buffalo Bill: Charles Eldridge Griffin in Europe: 1903–1906." *Palimpsest: Journal of the State Historical Society of Iowa* 54, no. 1 (Jan.–Feb. 1973): 2–14.

Griffin, Charles E. *Griffin's Book of Wonders.* New York: Charles E. Griffin, 1887.

———. *Traveling with a Circus: A History of Hunting's, N.Y.,*

Cirque Curriculum for Season 1888. New York: Van Fleet, 1888.

———. *How to Charm Snakes.* New York: Charles E. Griffin, 1890.

———. *How to Use Dumb Bells.* New York: Charles E. Griffin, 1890.

———. *Griffin's Magic Primer, or, First Book of Conjuring.* New York: Charles E. Griffin, 1896.

———. *How to Be a Contortionist, or, Bending Made Easy.* New York: Charles E. Griffin, 1896.

———. *Satan's Supper, or, Secrets of a Fire King.* New York: Van Fleet, 1896.

———. *Griffin's Wonder Worker, or, Second Book of Conjuring.* New York: Charles E. Griffin, 1897.

———. *The Showman's Book of Wonders.* New York: Charles E. Griffin, 1897.

———. *A Conjuror's Workshop.* New York: Charles E. Griffin, 1903.

———. *Four Years in Europe With Buffalo Bill.* Albia IA: Stage, 1908.

Kasson, Joy S. *Buffalo Bill's Wild West: Celebrity, Memory, and Popular History.* New York: Hill & Wang, 2000.

Kroes, Rob et al., eds. *Cultural Transmissions and Receptions: American Mass Culture in Europe; European Contributions to American Studies,* Vol. 25. New York: Ransom, 1993.

Lukens, John, and George S. Coleman. *The Sanger Story.* London: Hodder & Staughton, 1956.

Maddra, Sam A. *Hostiles?: The Lakota Ghost Dance and Buffalo Bill's Wild West.* Norman: University of Oklahoma Press, 2006.

Marill Escudé, Josep. *Aquell hivern . . . L'espectacle de Buffalo Bill a Barcelona*. Palma de Mallorca: Hesperus, 1998.

Moses, Lester G. *Wild West Shows and the Images of American Indians, 1883–1933*. Albuquerque: University of New Mexico Press, 1996.

Noble, James. *Around the Coast with Buffalo Bill: The Wild West in Yorkshire and Lincolnshire*. Beverley, UK: Hutton, 1999.

Parker, Lew. *Odd People I Have Met*. n.p.: n.d. (1910?).

Polacsek, John F. "Seeing the Elephant: The McCaddon International Circus of 1905." *Bandwagon: Journal of the Circus History Society* 26, no. 5 (1982): 13–20.

Reiss, Benjamin. *The Showman and the Slave: Race, Death, and Memory in Barnum's America*. Cambridge MA: Harvard University Press, 2001.

Reddin, Paul. *Wild West Shows*. Urbana: University of Illinois Press, 1999.

Russell, Don. *The Lives and Legends of Buffalo Bill*. Norman: University of Oklahoma Press, 1960.

Rydell, Robert W., and Rob Kroes. *Buffalo Bill in Bologna: The Americanization of the World, 1869–1922*. Chicago: University of Chicago Press, 2005.

Sanger, George. *Seventy Years a Showman: My Life and Adventures in Camp and Caravan the World Over (with an introduction by Kenneth Grahame)*. 1908; rpt. London: Wayfarer's Library, 1927.

Saxon, Arthur H. *P. T. Barnum: The Legend and the Man*. New York: Columbia University Press, 1995.

Sears, John. "Bierstadt, Buffalo Bill, and the Wild West in Europe." In *Cultural Transmissions and Receptions: American*

Mass Culture in Europe: European Contributions to American Studies, Volume XXV, edited by Rob Kroes et al., 3–15. New York: Ransom, 1993.

Standing Bear, Luther. *My People the Sioux.* 1928; rpt. Lincoln: University of Nebraska Press, 1975.

Stern, Giorgio. *Buffalo Bill a Trieste.* Trieste, Italy: La Mongolfiera, 1994.

Warren, Louis S. *Buffalo Bill's America: William Cody and the Wild West Show.* New York: Alfred A. Knopf, 2005.

Watkins, Harvey L. *The Tour of 1897: A Daily Record of the Triumphs of The Barnum & Bailey Greatest Show on Earth.* Buffalo NY: Courier, 1897.

Whetmore, Helen Cody. *Last of the Great Scouts.* Chicago: Duluth, 1899.

Whyte, George R. *The Dreyfus Affair: A Chronological History.* Basingstoke, UK: Palgrave MacMillan, 2008.

In the Papers of William F. "Buffalo Bill" Cody series

Four Years in Europe with Buffalo Bill
By Charles Eldrige Griffin
Edited and with an introduction by Chris Dixon